I GIVE MYSELF AWAY

GEORGE PANTAGES

Copyright © 2017

I Give Myself Away

By George Pantages

Printed in the United States of America

ISBN 978-0-9989538-0-9

All rights reserved solely by the author. The author guarantees all contents are original and do not infringe upon the legal rights of any other person or work. No part of this book may be reproduced in any form without the permission of the author.

Unless stated otherwise, all Scripture references come from the NKJV translation of the Bible, copyright © 2006 Thomas Nelson.

KJV. Copyright © 2006 by Thomas Nelson.

George Pantages Ministries

Cell 512 785-6324
geopanjr@yahoo.com
Georgepantages.com

TABLE OF CONTENTS

Chapter 1
I GIVE MYSELF AWAY …………………… 13

Chapter 2
I MUST DECREASE ………………………. 27

Chapter 3
O HOW HE LOVES YOU AND ME …….. 43

Chapter 4
BY INVITATION ONLY ………………….. 57

Chapter 5
IF AND ONLY IF ………………………..…. 77

Chapter 6
INCONVENIENCED ……………………..… 91

Chapter 7
A GODLY SORROW …………………….… 105

Chapter 8
PHYSICIAN HEAL THYSELF …………... 119

Chapter 9
IT'S NEVER TOO LATE ……………………. 133

DEDICATION

When my life was in disarray back in 2008, Pastor Raul Orozco was there to lend a helping hand. If you didn't know him and met him for the first time you would never believe he is the pastor of the largest church of the UPCI, hands down. He oversees 28 churches with approximately 7,300 members. He is also the National Spanish Director for the UPCI. But you wouldn't know it by his persona because he exudes humility and he doesn't let his success go to his head. In the short time I congregated in his church I was able to glean much understanding from his counseling. He was always very encouraging and he lifted me up at a time that I needed it so desperately. Now as I have moved from California to Texas, I observe from afar, and I still like what I see. Thank you, Pastor for all you are and for all you do, it is greatly appreciated.

DEDICATION

In the Christian life, we are all brothers and sisters. Every once in a while, you will find a good friend and even more rare is to find a really GOOD friend. That's what Gerry Marin is to me. He not only is a man of integrity, but is also a man of faith. He preaches the word with fervor and without compromise. But the real reason why we are friends is because he is flat-out HILARIOUS. When my wife and I get together with him and his family, I bow out to let him take control of the conversation. There is never a dull moment in the Marin household and I always seem to leave them completely renewed and refreshed to continue my journey. Thank you, Pastor Marin for you being the way you are for you truly uplift my soul!

INTRODUCTION

If only life could be lived without any inconveniences, that really would be Heaven. But the fact of the matter is we live in an imperfect world, with imperfect people. We not only have to endure inconveniences we must not let them get the best of us. Because this Christian life can at times rub people the wrong way, we must be prepared to confront those who oppose us with grace and patience.

When the Lord asked me to write this book, I was inconvenienced to the Nth degree. After writing the last book I had pretty much exhausted all of my resources. To continue writing and to create a new book was going to be more than challenging. Besides the need to do research for the first time being frightening, I also had to battle against my thought processes continuing to be somewhat deficient. I still have not fully recovered from my stroke and consequently I am slowed down constantly by losing my train of thought. Was this inconvenience enough to make me stop writing? Not a chance!

Inconveniences, with the help of the Holy Ghost are no longer nuisances. If we accept them with the right attitude, then they can be used to help us win the lost. When those who do not know Christ observe our "cool under pressure" attitude, then they too will hunger for what we have received through Christ.

The only way to live for Christ, is to have Him be in control of every facet of your life. You have already decided to live for God. Now, surrender it all to Him and GIVE YOURSELF AWAY!

APPRECIATION

I would like to take the time to appreciate the following people for their contribution on the publication of this book:

    Michelle Levigne – Editor
    Mlevigne.com

    Luis Villegas – Book Cover Design
    DPIXO Graphics, Dpixo.com

    Maria Pantages – Typesetting

Your professionalism and expertise rang true throughout the entire process, making my writing a whole lot better than it really is.

First, give yourself to God: He can do more with you than you can.

Unknown

Chapter 1

I GIVE MYSELF AWAY

But made Himself (Jesus) of no reputation, taking the form of a bondservant, and coming in the likeness of men.
                                        (Philippians 2:7)

There is an Old Testament law that has fascinated me for the longest time. It deals with people who have gotten into debt and cannot pay back their debt. If this were the case, the creditor could claim the debtor as a slave until the debt was paid, or up to six years of time. All the rights and privileges the debtor was accustomed to were taken away and he did only what he was told. It did not matter how unfair or difficult the task was, he was obligated to do anything and everything the creditor asked of him. In other words, the creditor would become the master and the debtor would become a slave.

> *If you buy a Hebrew servant, he shall serve six years; and in the seventh he shall go out free and pay nothing*
> (Exodus 21:2)

Stipulated in the law was an "out clause." After six years of labor, the slave had the option of leaving the master's house, or if he was happy in his new surroundings, he also had the option to stay.

> *And when you send him away free from you, you shall not let him go away empty-handed; you shall supply him liberally from your flock, from your threshing floor, and from your winepress. From what the LORD your God has blessed you with, you shall give to him.*
> (Deuteronomy 15:13-14)

Outlandish Demands

These demands given by the Lord to the master appeared outlandish, if not unfair. Whatever amount of money still owed, whether great or small, was to be written off and did not need to be repaid. At times, an unattainable balance of debt was zeroed out by the mercy of God. It is such a wonderful example of how far God's hand extends to those who are in need. For we know that His mercy will always trump sin, bringing blessing into our lives that we did not deserve. If the writing off of the debt appeared unfair to the master, the good fortune of the slave only got better when told that if he chose to leave the master, he could do so without the master's permission. His master would be obligated to empty out a part of his storehouse so that the slave would not leave empty-handed. By law, the slave would receive provisions that would allow him to start over with enough to make his "do-over" a complete success. Whether he was a good servant or not, hard-working or lazy, the blessing would fall under the category of "liberal" and the master had no choice in the matter.

Another Option

But there was another option given to the slave, and in the eyes of many outsiders, this option was ridiculous. This slave was given the option to also stay under the master's care. What would cause a man to give up his rights to live a life of freedom and continue a life restricted in bondage? In the process of living under the supervision of the master, a mutual love relationship was formed and grew to great proportions. It grew in such a manner that this relationship could no longer be based on legal obligation, but one out of love. Unbelievable to most people, the slave made a decision to stay because he wanted to.

His new life in the master's house was nothing like what he had envisioned. He had heard stories of abusive masters, and when he initially began to pay his debt, those atrocities were in the back of his mind. But his master was nothing like the abusive masters he had heard about. Over a period of time, working together, a bond of trust was formed like he had never experienced. Daily working hand-in-hand allowed the slave to see, close up, the special qualities and virtues of the man he called his boss. There was no being taken advantage of, no overworking, much less lording over a man who by law could not defend himself. After a period of time, he truly believed that the master had his best interests in mind when he was ordered to do particular tasks. As the relationship grew, so did his respect and appreciation for the master, and consequently he never felt like a slave. In his eyes, he felt more like family, and even at times as if he were in actuality the master's son. Not only was he well taken care of, but if in the time under the care of the master he had children, his wife and children were taken care of as lovingly as he was.

On to Bigger and Better Things

As the master continually demonstrated his love for the entire family, the slave came to the conclusion that living in this manner was an unexpected blessing. He too found himself changing in ways he thought were not possible. He was becoming more loving himself, more patient and kind, not to say that peace of mind was now making its way into his heart. With his new lease on life, he wanted to continue his ascent to bigger and better things for his family, so he worked tirelessly to be the successful man he knew he could become, pleasing his master in the process.

To get to this point, he knew he needed to make adjustments, because the life before him was nothing like the life he lived in the past. At first when the master tried to explain the ins and outs of how he wanted the household to be run and what he expected of the slave himself, much of what was told him did not make any sense at all. But there was something inside him that said, "Give it a chance, who knows, maybe it just might work." So the decision was made to "walk by faith and not by sight," and little by little, he began to understand the intricacies of how and why this household was run in a particular way. What was not evident to him at the outset became crystal clear with time, and it allowed him to appreciate the master even more. What a privilege it was to sit at the master's feet, learning ways to live a more blessed life.

Now that it all made sense to him, the thoughts of this restrictive lifestyle being nothing more than a form of legalism could be discarded without losing sleep. This freedom allowed him to live in peace, a peace that had escaped him his entire life. What was not understandable in the beginning became clear and pointed to a better way. With this new mindset controlling his new lifestyle, he could now overtake the shallow and self-centered motives in his past life and kick them to the curb. He came to the conclusion that although he had every right to leave when this six years of incarceration were over, it was in his best interests to stay.

When Others Have Left

There have been some in the past who, when given the choice to leave, took a leap of faith and had left the master's house. They were determined to prove they were right in leaving and at the same time very capable of making it on their own. There were others who had left the master's house who were somewhat wishy-washy in their service to God. Without any sure footing, they left and never again were able to find the comfort and peace they once experienced in the master's house. There is another group of people who had made the decision to leave, but when they were not able to find what they were looking for in their newfound freedom, they in turn blamed the master for their shortcomings. They would never admit that it was a mistake to leave the master's house; nevertheless they had become bitter toward the master. Finally, there was another group that had left the master's house, and in actuality they had succeeded in their new venture away from the master's house. They continued in their service to God, but somewhat with a watered down effect. In their eyes, they had eliminated all of the needless baggage that was holding them back in the kingdom of God. But in reality, eliminating the "so-called" unnecessary parts in their service to the Lord, they failed to realize that in God's house everything is integrated. We cannot take the same approach in serving God that is taken when one tries to assemble a bike without the instructions, not knowing what to do with the spare parts when the bike is supposedly completed. A bike, or anything else left in that manner will eventually fall apart. This, my friends, is a classic example of PRESUMPTION (behavior perceived as arrogant, transgressing the limits of what is permitted or appropriate).

Understanding Both Sides

Now that we understand both sides of the equation, let's look at the pros and cons of these decisions. These are the pros the slave (soon to become a love slave) would consider:

First of all, with the decision made to stay where he is at now, the master would provide a permanent job for life. This job included room and board for both him and his family. A decision to stay also meant that every need of life was taken care of for the love slave by the master. Finally, and most importantly, the relationship between the two changed from master and slave to friends. Whereas before the decision was made to stay, the relationship could be considered already "friendly," the actual decision to stay would make it official and binding. When the decision to stay was actually made, it had to be made in a public setting. The piercing of an ear would make it official.

> *Then his master shall bring him to the judges. He shall also bring him to the door, or to the doorpost, and his master shall pierce his ear with an awl; and he shall serve him forever.*
> (Exodus 21:6)

This piercing of the ear began a new covenant relationship based on love alone and was one of deep and abiding commitment. This is almost like a fairytale, one in which the characters, downtrodden for years, living in despair, find themselves with a golden opportunity to make such a great change in their future. "Living happily ever after" becomes a reality, one that brings such joy and relief to the recipient.[1]

Old Testament vs New Testament

To make any sense of the love relationship in the Old Testament between a master and his "love slave," we can fast-forward to the New Testament for a similar example. On His road to Calvary, Jesus took a path that few leaders would even think about taking.

> *But made Himself (Jesus) of no reputation, taking the form of a bondservant, and coming in the likeness of men.*
> (Philippians 2:7)

Is it any wonder that the reception Jesus received was such a cold one? He caught them completely off guard, bringing His ministry to the world in a manner that was not majestic. At no time in their history had the Jewish royalty presented themselves like common folk. But here He was, front and center, in His shameful glory, looking more like a pauper than a royal king who would take them out of captivity. Not only did He not look the part, His purpose in life would be accomplished by serving. Serving? A king does not rule by serving. He is admired, respected and successful by ruling, and ruling with a firm hand.

> *"Just as the Son of Man did not come to be served, but to serve, and to give His life a ransom for many."*
>
> (Matthew 20:28)

The Stage Has Been Set

The stage had been set for a paradigm shift. The pattern to follow in the future was unfolding right before their eyes and was clear-cut. To be successful in the kingdom of God, you had to serve and give, just like Jesus did. So, what would be the underlying benefit?

> *No longer do I call you servants, for a servant does not know what his master is doing; but I have called you friends, for all things that I heard from My Father I have made known to you.*
>
> (John 15:15)

The door to spiritual intimacy had been unlocked and the Lord could now become... *a friend who sticks closer than a brother.* (Prov. 18:24) But one last litmus test had to be passed. When James and John asked the Lord a pointed and somewhat selfish question, the Lord responded with a question of His own.

"You do not know what you ask. Are you able to drink the cup that I drink, and be baptized with the baptism that I am baptized with?"

(Mark 10:38)

In other words, will suffering for Christ become the characteristic people will use to describe your relationship with God? As much as they wanted to impress the Lord with a positive answer, Christ knew it would be a daunting task to complete. Yet, suffering in and for the kingdom of God is what serving the Lord is all about. A heavy dose of suffering will always keep pride in its place, not permitting it to rear its ugly head, destroying everything in its path.

U.S. citizens, including the Christians, as a whole, are very selfish and not easily motivated to struggle for the niceties in this life. Each generation following World War II has slowly lost its bearings as to what is important in life, especially in the kingdom of God. So much has been accumulated without much painstaking effort, much of which was just given, that this generation honestly believes everything that their heart desires should be handed to them on a silver platter. Any discomfort in life is viewed as unnecessary, one that cramps their hedonistic lifestyle, which of course they can do without.

A Classic Example of Suffering

But what can we learn from prior generations that will help us get back on the straight and narrow? What can we glean from our parents and/or grandparents that will help us gain our bearings in our attempt to be pleasing to our God? I would like to share a testimony I heard back in the early 70's, preached by a great man of God who has gone on to be with the Lord. Pastor Merrill Ewing from

I Give Myself Away

Louisiana preached this message at a Landmark conference in Stockton, California. The message itself zeroes in on the extremes people will go through to understand what it is to suffer. It has been over forty years from the last time I actually heard this message on tape. Nevertheless, the impact I feel today, so many years later, is even greater than when I heard it for the first time. See what you think.

After a period of time, the burdens the missionaries carried who were sent from the United States kept growing by leaps and bounds. There was a particular Korean woman, who at the time showed great interest in the gospel. She was pregnant and just about ready to give birth to her child. If you know anything about the country of Korea, then you understand that its winters can be very brutal. It just so happened that this Korean mother was due to give birth during the wintertime. As the gospel began to penetrate her heart, she made the decision to give her life to the Lord and was excited to have the opportunity of raising her child in Christianity.

The village she lived in was somewhat distant from where the missionaries actually lived. It would take them some time to get to the village, but because of such great need to tell these Koreans about Jesus, the sacrifice in their eyes was very minimal. As the story goes, that particular winter was extremely fierce. The hospital that was to deliver the baby was quite a distance from the village the woman lived in. If inclement weather were the order of the day, it would have made it extremely difficult for her to arrive safely. Because she did not own an automobile, she was completely dependent on the missionaries to get her to the hospital in time. That wasn't even the worst part of her situation. Neither did she own

I Give Myself Away

a telephone to use to make that call when she was ready to give birth.

On the day she finally gave birth to her little boy, one of the worst snowstorms hit that area of Korea. Waiting as long as she could to see if the storm would break, she made a decision that would ultimately take her life. Because she could not communicate with the missionaries, she decided to make a gallant effort to reach the hospital on foot. As the blizzard grew more intense, she figured she had gone as far she could and her efforts to save her baby in this kind of weather were hopeless. She then found a bridge to hide under, and shortly after that, to her complete horror, her water bag broke. The Holy Ghost calmed her enough to deliver the baby safely. Still not out of the woods, she had to figure out a way to keep the baby warm, or her efforts to save him would be futile. She did something that came naturally to a mother trying to save one of her children. She took off her overcoat, wrapped the baby inside, and laid over him, using her body heat to keep him alive.

Somehow the missionaries decided to go to her village, and when they could not find her, began an all-out search to locate her. They finally found her still covering her baby with the warmth of her body, but by that time she had frozen to death. The missionaries took them both, and after a heart-wrenching funeral, took the little Korean baby into their household. They wanted to make sure as he grew that he was aware of the great sacrifice his mom had made for him to live. It was something constantly on his mind, and he prayed that he would never forget why he still had the breath of life.

One day, the missionaries lost track of him. It was during wintertime, and in this case it was one of those winters that were extremely harsh. He was nowhere to be found, and of course the missionaries were running around frantically, trying to find him before the weather would take his life. After a period of searching throughout the area, the Lord spoke to the missionary, saying where he could find the little boy. Immediately they went to the cemetery where the mother of this boy was buried. He was about eleven years old at this time, truly able to understand the great sacrifice his mother gave for him to live. When the missionaries found him, he was sprawled over his mother's grave, without a shirt, shivering from the cold, and uttering words like this:

"Mama, was it this cold the day you died for me?"

"Mama, how did it feel knowing if help did not come in time you would freeze to death?"

"Mama, I'm freezing out here. Can you hear me? Mama, I would do anything to help you understand just how much I love you."

The missionaries found him in time before his body was completely frostbitten. He was willing to give his life to repay the love and kindness his mother showed to him.

God's Ultimate Plan for Us

Now, let me get something straight here. The Lord is not asking any of us to die a painful death for Him. What indeed He is asking is that you and I live for Him. His ultimate plan to keep us in check, after receiving countless blessings over and over in our lifetime, will be through our suffering in Him.

On judgment day, when all is said and done and we are brought before the throne of God to receive whatever rewards we have gained through a lifetime of service and suffering, I think ultimately we could agree with the words the apostle Paul also wisely wrote.

> *For this reason I also suffer these things; nevertheless I am not ashamed, for I know whom I have believed and am persuaded that He is able to keep what I have committed to Him until that Day.*
> (2 Timothy 1:12)

Because I have such a great desire to make a difference in the kingdom of God, I will gladly… GIVE MYSELF AWAY.

Nothing sets a person so much out of the devil's reach as humility
Jonathan Edwards

Chapter 2

I MUST DECREASE

He must increase, but I must decrease.

(John 3:30)

Diminishing returns is something I remember learning about in my college days, when I was majoring in business administration. There is not much that I technically remember about the two economics classes I was required to take. But, for some reason the phrase "diminishing returns" has stuck in my memory even to this day some forty-odd years later. By definition, a diminishing return is a point at which the level of profits gained is less than the amount of money invested.[2] Of course, the goal of any company in business is to make a profit. The initial goal, when expenses are higher than profits, is to first get to a breakeven point where spending is brought under control. It is then that adjustments are made to consistently make sure that profits are always higher than expenses.

Diminishing Returns and Christianity

What do diminishing returns have to do with the Christian life? All you must do is look at the Scripture above and conclude that it is everything. The more God is in control of your life, the better servant of God you become. When Christ is at the center of everything you do, things fall into place and a quiet confidence continues to grow, knowing that Jesus has your back. He always has your best interests in mind and whether you believe it or not, He wants you to succeed. He thinks about us more than we give Him credit for. Look what Jeremiah has to say about this.

> *For I know the thoughts that I think toward you, says the LORD, thoughts of peace and not of evil, to give you a future and a hope.*
>
> (Jeremiah 29:11)

Diminishing returns in our spiritual lives become the springboard God uses to bless us in ways He has always wanted. As the sin, bad habits, ungodly conversation, and impure thoughts are covered by the blood of the Lamb, the Lord has the opportunity to bless us in ways far beyond our comprehension. When we arrive at that breakeven point, allowing God complete control from that day forward, Satan no longer has dominion over us. Just like the "love slave" mentioned in Chapter 1, there is a new lease on life, allowing us to pursue bigger and better things without a sense of guilt and/or condemnation.

> *There is therefore now no condemnation to those who are in Christ Jesus, who do not walk according to the flesh, but according to the Spirit.*
> (Romans 8:1)

Apostle John's Diminishing Life

One of the great men of God who lived a life of diminishing returns was the apostle John. Although the Scripture we find in John 3:30 was said by John the Baptist, we can conclude that the apostle John wrote it, gleaning from the eyewitness experiences he had with John the Baptist, who was his first spiritual mentor. The apostle was constantly diminishing his life so he could live up to the calling as one of Christ's disciples.

Before he met Christ, he did not live up to his name. The Hebrew meaning for John was a dove, implying the grace of the Lord.[3] Initially, he did not come anywhere near that definition. It would be one that he would slowly accept, making the necessary changes to live up to that name. As a follower of John the Baptist, his character was more like his first mentor. He was single-minded, brash, and bold. Like his mentor, he would take this world by storm and with a made-up mind would not allow anything, or anyone, to get in his way.

Revisionist history paints a completely different picture, in that he is viewed as a soft-spoken, quiet, and unpretentious man. Because he was the youngest of the disciples chosen by Christ, he was presumed to be lacking in experience and know-how compared to the other disciples. The fact of the matter was that John was trained in the art of fishing and was hardened by living a rugged lifestyle. In reality, he was just as prepared to lead the church as were Peter or Paul. Fishing exposed him to inclement weather, so taking great risks was a normal part of the job. He learned to be quick on his feet and decisive in giving orders. Dillydallying in making important decisions could ultimately result in death, so he was aware of the fact that great responsibility was placed on his shoulders. His leadership skills were developed early in life, preparing him for a ministry that would be even more difficult. Because of his strength as well as his tenderness, Jesus would come to lean on him for support and trust, both literally and figuratively. He demonstrated great instincts and uncanny insights in so many different areas that far exceeded the other disciples. He had the foresight of a prophet as well, and it was a great asset as he became the spokesperson for the church after the deaths of the other apostles.

John had the unique ability to defer these qualities until the most opportune time. I don't believe he minded anyone thinking less of him because he understood the giftings Christ had placed in his life, and was not in any hurry to show them off. Therefore he was confident in his abilities even though they were hidden from the rest of the world. I believe because he was the youngest of the apostles it made it a bit easier to defer to the rest of the followers of Jesus. When it was the right time he would step up to the plate, accept his responsibility and be successful in it. He was very much like Jesus in this respect in that Jesus had to wait 30 years in silence before it was time to move to the head of the class and show the world that He truly was the coming Messiah. When you have the ability to help correct a wrong and make it right, you instinctively want to press forward. Jesus limited Himself in that respect successfully and it would be a lesson that John would have to learn as well. Waiting patiently for your turn is not a virtue so easily acquired, but John was willing to make those adjustments to be used by God.

John the Baptist became his first mentor and John was completely captivated by this great man of God. The Baptist was so confident, so fiery in his presentation of the word. He had the ability to motivate anyone and everyone within earshot of his voice. Something had to be extremely different about this man of God to be able to have the ability of drawing great crowds in the desert. There was nothing fancy or flashy about him, as he dressed in camel hair and demonstrated great humility. But there was something about the way he spoke that could lure John to take a closer look at the Christ the Baptist was preaching about. I am sure he had envisioned himself working side-by-side with the Baptist to win a lost world to the Lord. What a privilege it would have been to closely watch this man of God preaching anointed messages that would convince the masses to convert to Christianity. Furthermore, if he could become like the Baptist and follow in his footsteps, that truly would be a dream come true.

The Face of Christianity is About to Change

Of course, the Baptist understood his days as the face of Christianity were temporary because he was sent into the world to prepare the way for the Messiah. I am sure many of his followers were so enamored with this fearless, unrelenting man of God that stepping aside for another, in their eyes, would be blasphemous. So, to make the transition easier and clear to those in his audience, at the time when he baptized Jesus he quoted these immortal words:

He must increase, but I must decrease.

(John 3:30)

Whether John truly understood the words of the Baptist that day or not, they would later become a part of his life as long as he lived. You could pretty much say that these words would become a sort of mantra of the apostle John that would clearly define the rest of his ministry. After the beheading of the Baptist, these words made more sense, so taking them to heart, he made a gallant effort to follow Jesus and would make them his own.

The Molding Begins

First item on the agenda meant he had to be made aware of his shortcomings, so Christ could mold him into the man he was later to be. Jesus then would rename him and his brother, and from that day forward they would be known as "Boanerges," which meant Sons of Thunder. They both had anger and attitude issues, which caused them to be intolerant and resentful of abuses. In their eyes, it was easier to call down fire from heaven than to remain meek. These types of reactions to people who were not on the same spiritual level as they were would not be tolerated by Jesus. They would have to learn to bite their tongues, grin and bear it. Until their blinded eyes were opened to see a lack of humility in their lives, they would never be useful in God's kingdom. He brought that to their attention when He stated this to James and John.

..."*You do not know what manner of spirit you are of.*
(Luke 9:55)

What a slap in the face, not to mention a shot to their egos. Right when they felt as if they were making headway, the bubble was burst and they humbly returned to square one. Could it be that John also could hear the voice of his mentor helping him to remember what was essential to becoming a competent servant to Christ? *I must decrease, I must decrease, I must decrease...* It must have driven him crazy, but at the same time helped him come to the realization that becoming Christ-like was no easy task.

A Confidant of The Master

Little by little, he became a confidant of the Master.[4] The Scriptures tell us that he, along with Peter and James, became a part of Christ's inner circle. The Lord would share with them wisdom from His heart that He did not share with the other disciples. On at least four different occasions, those three experienced things that the rest were not privy to. Only they were eyewitnesses to the raising of Jairus' daughter from the dead. When Jesus went to the mount of Transfiguration, those three saw Him transfigured in His glory. They were so startled that they did not know how to react and muttered things to the Lord that really made no sense. Then John, along with Peter, was commanded by the Lord to find a place to make preparation for the "Last Supper." Lastly, they saw Jesus in agony in the Garden of Gethsemane. Never had they seen anyone pray so intensely that the sweat shed that night appeared as drops of blood.

A Spiritual "Consentido"

From this inner circle, John occupied the chief place in the heart of Christ. John was "the one whom Jesus loved." I know it appeared ludicrous to believe Christ played favorites, but I would like to share with you something that is very common in the Hispanic culture. Every Hispanic family has what is called a "CONSENTIDO." It is a son or daughter who holds first place in the heart of one or both parents. Understand that this place was not given to that child by the parents themselves. It was a place won by the child by kissing up. How is this possible? The CONSETIDO was always hovering over the parents. Any time a chore or an errand had to be done, they were right by the parent's side, and many times by default were asked to do that chore. Meanwhile, knowing that the parents would at one time or another ask all their children to do something they really didn't like doing, the others had an inner radar that kept them far away from the parents, especially when work must be done. On the other hand, because the "CONSENTIDO" was always nearby, when it came to an extra blessing being doled out, guess who's first in line for that blessing? That is right, the "CONSENTIDO." Although God does not play favorites in His kingdom, what He does have in comparison is what we call "INTIMATES." These are children of God who are always seeking God's face. To them, serving God means putting forth a diligent effort not only to find God, but also to minister to His needs.

> *But without faith it is impossible to please Him, for he who comes to God must believe that He is, and that He is a rewarder of those who diligently seek Him.*
>
> (Hebrews 11:6)

That was John's place. He made the initial move and won the Lord's heart. Always remaining close, there was a notion that perhaps his relationship with God would intensify and that if he was constantly in His presence, he would glean more spiritual insight from Jesus. This was a man who truly understood the heartbeat of God.

Being Loved by God

To get the full impact of what it means to be loved by God in this manner, we should consider this:

For whom the LORD *loves He corrects, just as a father the son in whom he delights.*

(Proverbs 3:12)

His correction can be brutally painful in that it can emotionally find its way into the deepest depths of one's heart. Like a master surgeon, He has the ability to find the root of our deficiencies, making us aware, subtly yet effectively, to rid ourselves of the things that hinder our walk with God.

Case in point: when Christ asked the three (Peter, James, and John) to pray while He found a more private place in the Garden of Gethsemane. When He returned after a period, He found them asleep. What He said next to them was a literal wake-up call.

"What! Could you not watch with Me one hour?

(Matthew 26:40)

He didn't wait for a response, but I am sure the embarrassment they felt, especially John, would not be soon forgotten. I can imagine John kicking himself, wondering how this could have possibly happened. After all, what separated him from the rest of the disciples was his relationship with Christ, and for this, his actions were unacceptable. He knew that Peter and James could easily put this experience behind them, but not John, who was far more sensitive than the other two. In the back of his mind, there had to be a way to make this up to the Lord, and this would nag him until he made it right.

An Opportunity Presents Itself

That opportunity came just a short period after. The scene now was on the hill of Golgotha, and Jesus was being readied for His crucifixion. He had been whipped unmercifully, within an eyelash of death. His back now looked more like spaghetti, with a loss of blood that would have killed anyone else. The beating He ultimately took left Him physically unrecognizable.

> *Just as there were many who were appalled at him -- his appearance was so disfigured beyond that of any human being and his form marred beyond human likeness.*
> (Isaiah 52:14 NIV)

Jesus demonstrated His power of forgiveness with what happened next. John was one of the few disciples who made their way to the crucifixion area. As he moved amongst the crowd, he found Mary, the mother of Jesus, front and center. I am sure one of the reasons he approached the cross so closely was to console Mary. At this time, Jesus did something unexpected that would allow John to know that the Messiah was not holding any grudges over his failure in the garden of Gethsemane. Jesus tenderly committed the care of His mother to John.

When Jesus therefore saw His mother, and the disciple whom He loved standing by, He said to His mother, "Woman, behold your son!" Then He said to the disciple, "Behold your mother!" And from that hour that disciple took her to his own home.

(John 19:26-27)

All of John's training in the presence of the Lord had fully prepared him for this next assignment. The burden of caring for the Master's mother was placed on the right shoulders because he was now ready.

Life After Christ's Death

Life after Christ's death would bring a challenge into his life like no other he had experienced previously. He would have to take all his life lessons and apply them to his daily walk with God. It would prove to be quite useful, because John now would be given greater responsibility in the church. But, this would all be put on hold until the death of Mary, the mother of Jesus. This was approximately fourteen years later. In the meantime, he deferred his authority to Peter. There are at least three different portions of Scripture that bear this out. In the book of Acts chapter 3, at the healing of the lame man it is Peter who took the initiative to pray so the lame man was miraculously healed. It was also Peter who then explained to the high priest what had happened, while John took a backseat, backing him up with quiet support. Finally, when they made a trip to the area of Samaria (Acts 8:14), once again it was Peter who took charge of the situation and these Samaritans received the baptism of the Holy Ghost for the first time. During this fourteen-year period, it appeared that John's focus was on the care of Mary, the mother of Jesus, and when she died his ministry would blossom like no other time in his experience with God. Up until this time, John had become a quiet pillar of the Church.

Time to Step It Up

During this time frame, Peter and Paul were martyred for their faith and faithfulness to the Lord Jesus Christ. It was now time for John to step up, take on the leadership role of the church, and become the new face of Christianity. For all of the struggle John had endured to rid himself of the "Son of Thunder" label, now it was time to adjust his personality, stepping up into his new leadership responsibilities. Tradition tells us that John evangelized Asia Minor and was responsible for opening new churches in the areas of Smyrna, Philadelphia, and Laodicea. Later in his ministry, he was falsely accused in the city of Ephesus. He was then sent bound to Rome when, in trying to further the gospel, he was thrown into a cauldron of boiling oil. Unfortunately, for the leaders in Rome, his life was miraculously spared, and out of desperation they decided to send him to the island of Patmos to die in one of the most detestable prisons at that time.

I believe the Scripture that described Joseph's reaction to the misfortunes in his life would be a similar statement made by John.

> *But as for you, you meant evil against me; but God meant it for good, in order to bring it about as it is this day, to save many people alive.*
>
> (Genesis 50:20)

The Isle of Patmos

Being sent to the island of Patmos was pretty much a death sentence for those sent to this godforsaken island. By definition, the name Patmos means "my killing." It was a sterile, infertile island, unable to produce offspring or bear seeds. The extremely high cliffs made it impossible to escape, and consequently the morale of those encamped here was very low.[5] The grueling labor was backbreaking, not to mention strenuous and fatiguing. There was no escape from this death camp, nevertheless this was the best place John could have been sent to because it allowed him to enter a frame of mind that would be useful in writing the book of Revelation. It was written under the most demanding of circumstances, yet with a matchless fortitude of strength he completed his assignment. Any other man would have died under these circumstances and been bitter about it, but not John. In his eyes, it was an honor to write a book so profound and needful to the body of Christ, and any inconvenience in his life could not compare to the suffering of his Master. These lifelong, impossible challenges helped mold John into an unmovable force.

John's Other Books

As profound as the book of Revelation is, we must consider some of the other books this apostle wrote, to get a clearer picture of the things God revealed to him in ministry. The first epistle of John set the universal rules for the conduct of a Christian. Because living for Christ did not come anywhere near the life and lifestyles humanity lived before coming to know Christ, there had to be a standard set to help us become more like Jesus. Living in holiness and pureness of manners was essential to the continuation and growth of the Church. If ground rules would not have been set, I'm sure in time the instructions of Christ would have been put on the back burner and eventually dismissed as something that was relevant to those times only. He was very concerned that the Church as a whole would not become satisfied with empty Christianity. He tirelessly repeated these principles to make sure they would not be forgotten in future generations.

Love One Another

He practiced love fully, recommending this virtue to be the focal point of their service unto the Lord. If you take time to study the epistles he wrote, this concept is plainly evident in each and every one. Look how he warmly addressed the church in the same way: "Little children, love one another." This phrase is sprinkled throughout his epistles, earmarking its importance in the kingdom of God. By this we can tell he had come a long way from the days he was called a "son of thunder." Initially, he was raw and undisciplined, but the potential Jesus saw in him catapulted him to heights in God that he never thought were possible. The end of his life was altogether something different. The godlike qualities, coupled with the grace of the Lord, truly painted a beautiful picture of what this disciple's life was all about. We can go back into history and see what the grace of God had accomplished in his lifetime. First and foremost, he was the only apostle not to die a martyr's death. Tradition teaches us that every single apostle used mightily in the kingdom of God had his life taken away from him, and in most cases, violently. If you had been chosen to be an apostle of Christ, you would have to forfeit the normal way of life. Dying for the cause of Christ was the ultimate compliment and these apostles were up to the challenge. It would not deter them from spreading the gospel to the entire world and they were truly valiant to the end. This man of God, on the other hand, lived to the ripe old age of approximately ninety-six. The Lord enjoyed his fellowship so much that He found it hard to let him go. They saw eye-to-eye and heart-to-heart, forming a relationship that in the future would be difficult to duplicate. In the kingdom of God, those kind of relationships are few and far between. When you cultivate a relationship similar to the one Jesus and John had, you hold on, until you cannot hold on any longer.

If we take the concept of diminishing returns and apply them to our spiritual lives, it will break the curse by the blood of the Lamb. If we could borrow John the Baptist's words and keep them as our mantra, we would eventually get to a breakeven point by God's grace. Only then would our successes in our spiritual lives become like those in the life of John. Can you still hear the voice of John saying, *I must decrease, I must decrease, I must decrease…?* All I can say to that is that I too must continue to decrease as well.

How do I love thee? Let me count the ways.

Elizabeth Barrett Browning

Chapter 3

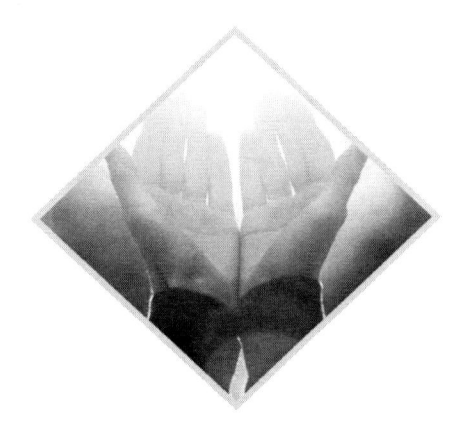

O HOW HE LOVES YOU AND ME

Now "If the righteous one is scarcely saved, where will the ungodly and the sinner appear?"
(1 Peter 4:18)

"Yes, I have loved you with an everlasting love; Therefore with lovingkindness I have drawn you.
(Jeremiah 31:3)

The opening statement by Peter has to unequivocally fall under the category of shocking. In the day and age we live in, the Church as a whole will not receive or accept the harsh words stated by the apostle. The world as we know it has become so overly sensitive it has overreacted to anyone and everyone who does not agree with their liberal agenda. Case in point: The Democratic Party in this country is having such a difficult time accepting that Donald Trump has been elected as the 45th president of the United States. The unrest in our country has grown to epic proportions and it doesn't appear to be letting up.

Mainstream Christianity also appears to have taken on the same approach in bringing salvation to a lost world. The salvation plan has been watered down so much that preachers of today are making it so easy to embrace a liberal lifestyle, when in turn they attack unmercifully people who hold onto the doctrines of the past. Truth be told, the righteous in the church today are scarcely saved. With that being said, where does that place those who do not know Jesus? We, as the body of Christ, must step up and help the rest of the world know that there is a God offering them eternal life. Pushing ourselves to become more Christ-like is the only way to arrive at that goal.

Jeremiah's Less Intimidating Words

Although Peter's words would appear very much daunting, intimidating those who fell under that category, Jeremiah's words are far less intimidating. In fact, the everlasting love Peter writes about is a love that is perpetual; i.e., ongoing, eternal, and forever. The Lord's love is a far cry from the love we express. Our love we express toward others is usually conditional, even when dealing with Christ. That means we love Him when He blesses us, and we are indifferent when He doesn't. Here is a good example of what I am talking about. In the animal kingdom, cats are a finicky bunch. They are somewhat stubborn, self-willed, and even at times prima donnas. If a cat decides it does not want to obey what its master is asking of it, it will just ignore you. Why? Because they appear to believe they are God's gift to humanity and that everyone should bow down to them. As Christians, most of us live like cats. We strut around as proud as a peacock, believing that the Lord is nothing more than a spiritual genie. There is a great attempt at misinterpreting Scripture so that God can give us anything to our hearts content

The dog, on the other hand, is completely different. His aim is to please his master, always excited to see them, wagging his tail perpetually, and licking their faces nonstop. Their energy says, "I want you to notice me by the attention I give to you." That's the kind of enthusiasm and excitement the Lord emits when we enter into our prayer closets to seek His face. God's greatest desire for us would be that we would return the favor and love Him in the same fashion.

> *But the hour is coming, and now is, when the true worshipers will worship the Father in spirit and truth; for the Father is seeking such to worship Him.*
>
> (John 4:23)

Finding worshipers is not an easy task. That is why the Scripture uses the word seeking. It is a search that is more intense because they are so difficult to find. But once they are found, the delight God finds in them reaches the stratosphere.

The Misunderstood Disciple

Now I would like to take the time to talk about one I call "the misunderstood disciple." His name is Judas Iscariot, and he is the most despised of all of the disciples. The book of Zechariah indirectly foretold his demise without naming him specifically.

> *Then I said to them, "If it is agreeable to you, give me my wages; and if not, refrain." So they weighed out for my wages thirty pieces of silver.*
>
> (Zechariah 11:12)

Because there was no name given, in reality it could have been any of the other disciples as well. Let's look at the resumes of some of the other disciples. Let's begin with Peter. He was extremely impulsive and decidedly presumptuous. In the following of Christ as a favored disciple, he denied the Lord three times. The denial was so reprehensible that on one occasion it included language that would make a sailor blush. What about the other two in Christ's inner circle, James and John? Their request after the mount of Transfiguration reeked with pride. Their request was plain and simple. "When we get to heaven, let both of us sit on either side of the throne." If that does not demonstrate pride, then nothing does. Remember, pride always comes before a fall. It was pride that knocked Lucifer from his place in heaven. The reaction of the disciples to the brothers' request could have started an avalanche of resentment, then causing the brothers to take the brunt of their error out on Jesus.

Judas' Label Came After the Betrayal

Judas' label as a thief and a traitor came after the betrayal. We must take into consideration that the book of Matthew, which documents the crucifixion of Christ, was written anywhere between eighty and ninety years after the death of the Lord. Not one of the disciples had accused Judas of being a traitor because he blended well with the others. Look at the reaction of the disciples when Jesus told them there was a traitor amongst His disciples.

Now as they were eating, He said, "Assuredly, I say to you, one of you will betray Me." And they were exceedingly sorrowful, and each of them began to say to Him, "Lord, is it I?"

(Matthew 26:21-22)

His future actions and/or intentions were so deeply hidden that no one amongst the rest of the disciples had a clue he was the culprit. His place in the pecking order of importance among the disciples was just below Peter, James, and John. He was chosen as the treasurer of the group, so he must have been highly respected to obtain that position. Understand that before the betrayal, he was part of a group that went out to preach the gospel, casting out demons and healing the sick (Luke 10:1). There was a spirituality about him that was glossed over when the accounts of his life focused only on his betrayal. As far as Christ was concerned, He made every effort to form a vessel of honor, but in the end it was to no avail. His past life did him no favors.

Judas' Greatest Enemy

His greatest enemy was his greatest strength, which was his analytical mind. I'm sure Jesus took this into consideration when He chose Judas to be the group's money keeper. He could analyze, calculate, and successfully project numbers to make Jesus' ministry look really good. He had the ability to play with numbers, using that ability to steal money from the treasury without getting caught. It was like taking candy from a baby, and his lack of remorse was preparing him for the betrayal of all betrayals. I believe his analytical mind and his success as a thief gave him a sense of superiority. I have seen in my own lifetime men of God who had no accountability in the finances of the church make themselves believe that money stolen from the church treasury was something they deserved. They did not take into consideration the harm these acts of thievery would cause the trusting congregation, and consequently carried on as if they had done nothing wrong.

Because of his keen intellect, the lessons on faith went completely over his head and confused him. Here's one of those Scriptures Jesus blurted out that I suppose could have caused Judas some agitation.

> *And He sat down, called the twelve, and said to them, "If anyone desires to be first, he shall be last of all and servant of all."*
>
> (Mark 9:35)

What kind of kingdom was this man trying to establish? Didn't He know that those in power ruled with an iron fist? How in the world did He expect to conquer the world if He was going to serve everybody? For analytical people, it's all about checks and balances. In the kingdom of God, there are occasions when 1+1 does not equal 2. Those are the kinds of problems that drive analytical people crazy. The way of the kingdom was too abstract for him, it was completely beyond his way of thinking. Whether Judas objected publicly to these lessons of faith or not, we cannot tell for sure, but these types of

Scriptures could have pushed him over a cliff. The simplicity of faith could never be embraced, which resulted in great insecurities that he would never be able to overcome.

Jesus' Relentless Pursuit

Knowing this, Jesus would not let Judas' mindset detour His desire to win him over to His side. Christ's first show of His everlasting love is found in Matthew 26:23.

He answered and said, "He who dipped his hand with Me in the dish will betray Me.

For many people reading this passage of Scripture, it shows that Jesus knew ahead of time that one of His disciples would betray Him. For me, I see it a little bit differently. I can see the Lord desperately reaching out to one of His closest followers. It was a call to repentance, if you will, and a shocking one at that. There are times even in our own spiritual lives when Jesus ruffles our feathers to wake us up to get back on track before it's too late. He does it so gracefully that it does not destroy our desire to make amends for our wrong. He does it so subtly that most of the brethren are not privy to our shortcomings that need to be fixed. That being said, after Jesus made this shocking statement, none of the other disciples had a clue as to whom Jesus was talking about.

Jesus Probes Deeper

Knowing that Judas did not respond to the first call, Jesus decided to probe even deeper and be more direct.

> *The Son of Man indeed goes just as it is written of Him, but woe to that man by whom the Son of Man is betrayed! It would have been good for that man if he had not been born." Then Judas, who was betraying Him, answered and said, "Rabbi, is it I?" He said to him, "You have said it."*
> (Matthew 26:24-25)

It was not enough to change his mind. Perhaps he felt he had already crossed that point of no return and consequently closed himself to the Master's plea. I can truthfully admit that in the past when I failed God in one manner or another, the desire to get back on track fell by the wayside. You feel as if you had stumbled so miserably that even the mercy of God could not extend as low as you had fallen. Then in your mind, you say, "Why should I make an attempt to get back on track when you know that eventually it will happen again?" It is at that point most people do not get back up again. At this point of despair and dejection, Satan was allowed to take control of his life and destroy him as he always wanted to.

A Final Appeal

Jesus made a final appeal to win back His friend. We find this appeal in Luke 22:48:

> *But Jesus said to him, "Judas, are you betraying the Son of Man with a kiss?"*

Jesus had to let Judas know that He was aware of what he was trying to do. He was hoping His statement would shock him enough to allow him to humble himself and repent before it was too late. Sadly to say, his kiss of death sealed his fate and he would never allow God's everlasting love to bring him to a place of peace. With the sign of betrayal in place, the soldiers took Jesus away to a mock trial and then brutally crucified Him illegally. Meanwhile, Judas came to his senses, realizing he had betrayed an innocent man. He was so flustered by his error that in his eyes life was not worth living, and he committed suicide. I suppose that for some reading the reenactment of Judas' betrayal, you have taken the position that he got what he deserved. I have come to this conclusion: Our condemnation of this man of God is hypocritical. It amazes me how we can see ourselves as being holy. I want you to know that there is a great divide between how we see ourselves and how God sees us. We can go back to the words of Peter, and must confess his words are quite sobering.

Peter's Sobering Words

Now "If the righteous one is scarcely saved, where will the ungodly and the sinner appear?"

(1 Peter 4:18)

What kind of people fall under the category of righteous? People who are upright, virtuous, upstanding, and principled. The group could also include people who are honorable, blameless, irreproachable and noble. This group upholds the highest standards of living anyone could ever hope to have. Yet in the eyes of God they are barely making it. Again, the statement was not made to condemn but to motivate us to bigger and better things. That includes all of us, every single one of us.

What people believe to be true and what reality is, is really quite different. When lay people look to those of us in ministry, they definitely have an unrealistic view of how we live our lives. They place us on such a high pedestal, it is truly unreasonable to believe that anyone could live on that level. In my over forty years of serving God, I have found out that many men and women who were held in high esteem were normal people with a propensity to fall into sin like anyone else. For a period of time, I worked at the headquarters of a particular denomination. As I had to at various times go to the archives to find information on certain people, I found out that their backgrounds were not squeaky clean as I thought, but at times tainted with past sins. Abuses in every area were forced to be dealt with, and I was so disheartened by my discovery.

My Confession

I would love to say that my life in the Lord is perfect, but it's not, and I would like to share something that happened to me recently. My wife and I only have one grandson, and initially it was difficult for me to accept him as family. I say that because he was born to my wife's son from a previous marriage. Now then, that should not have made a difference in how the little one should be loved. But what was bothering me so much was that none of my three children who are older than my stepsons have had any of their own. I know this should not have made a difference, but at the time of this writing I am already on the north side of sixty years old. For years I had to endure other grandparents talking about their grandchildren with such gratification that it appeared unfair to have to wait for that same experience. Just knowing that I would be reexperiencing the delight I had raising my children, with another opportunity to do a rewind with my grandchildren. I could not do that with the one and only grandchild God had given to us. I felt a twinge of jealousy when my wife would mention all the similarities she saw between her grandson and her son. All the while I was seething on the inside, and it slowly but surely began to show in my actions. I did not personally say anything bad to my grandson, but at best I was indifferent. Where the cruelty really reared its ugly head was in the conversations with my wife. When she tried to share with me her delight in her only grandson, who in her eyes looked exactly like her own son, I began to lash out. She was horrified by my reaction to her pride, yet at the same time I was hurting so badly on the inside, that I wanted her to hurt as well. What a horrible thing to have to admit, yet it was true. After a period of time, my wife became bitter as well. I could see that the marriage was beginning to go downhill, but even then I wasn't willing to change my attitude to let her off the hook. What made matters worse was the fact that during this time my ministry was growing in leaps and bounds. It made it so much easier for me to justify my wrong because it appeared I was not being judged for my sin. Yet I had forgotten the word of God when He decides to deal with disobedient children. God could have easily let the hammer fall on me and come to the rescue of my wife, who had not done anything wrong. But He didn't! It was this Scripture that came to mind, preparing me for what would come next.

Or do you despise the riches of His goodness, forbearance, and longsuffering, not knowing that the goodness of God leads you to repentance?

(Romans 2:4)

God was not condoning my indifference, He was trying to reach me with His profound love so that I could repent. When blessing me in my ministry could not do the trick, the Lord did something that I will never forget.

An Undeserved Wake-up Call

One day, my wife was enjoying some videos her son had sent of the baby playing at Chuck-E-Cheese. I remember when she called me over to look at them, hoping I would enjoy them as much as she. The video was taken showing the baby throwing a ball at a set of rings. The more balls he was able to directly connect inside of the rings, the bigger prize he was to win. Because I did not really want to see what was going on the Lord immediately spoke to me and said this, "Look at which arm he is using to throw the ball." As I looked at what God wanted me to see, I observed that he was throwing the balls left-handed. I immediately asked my wife if anyone in her family was left-handed. When she responded to me with an emphatic no, the Lord then spoke again. "You have been giving grief to your wife for the grandson I have given her. You have complained to me that I've not been fair, and although it's not time for any of your children to have ones of their own, I made him left-handed just like you." Immediately the tears began to stream down my cheeks, and I wanted to find a place to pray so I could repent. I could not understand why the Lord was being so merciful to me when I was truly being a jerk and did not deserve it. But, that is the kind of love the Lord demonstrates to all of His children, whether we deserve it or not. There is one last Scripture I would like to share that means the world to me.

A Favorite Scripture

… "Yes, I have loved you with an everlasting love;
Therefore with lovingkindness I have drawn you.
(Jeremiah 31:3)

We need not take the same path that Judas took. Jesus was willing to forgive him up until his betrayal at Calvary. If that be so, who then would have become the traitor? Knowing that the Scripture had to be fulfilled, someone else would have taken his place. Jesus just wanted to let him know how loved he was, and if he would have decided not to go with the betrayal, the Lord would have found another way for the Scripture to be fulfilled. For this we can be thankful, knowing HOW MUCH HE LOVES YOU AND ME!

I do not know how to explain it; I cannot tell how it is, but I believe angels have a great deal to do with the business of this world.

Charles H. Spurgeon

Chapter 4

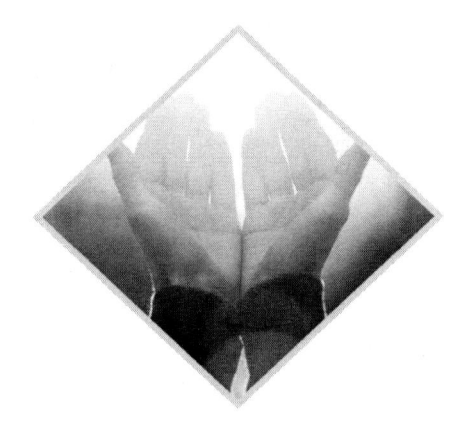

BY INVITATION ONLY

Are they not all ministering spirits sent forth to minister for those who will inherit salvation?

(Hebrews 1:14)

Any time a person accepts a new job position, part of the negotiations that play into convincing a prospective applicant to accept this job is a good benefits package. These packages usually include a great health and dental insurance plan, and at times companies are willing to pay for continuing education as well. Of course, sick pay is a given, and if available, the use of a company car. After a period of service in the company, the usual two-week vacation turns into three and perhaps four weeks. The closer that catches the interest of most people is the pension plan. Knowing that one will be taken care of nicely after retirement is important to most people.

The benefits package many companies offer does not even come close to the benefits package offered by our Lord. Because we have accepted the salvation He died on the cross for, our retirement package is simply heavenly. Eternal life in the presence of God cannot be bought or earned, as much as one would like to be able to do that. The grace of God is what allows us to be the beneficiaries of this eternal gift.

And I give them eternal life, and they shall never perish; neither shall anyone snatch them out of My hand.
(John 10:28)

An Untapped Source

There is an untapped source at our disposal that most Christians are not aware of. Ministering angels have been put in place for the benefit of the children of God. These angels provide the Kingdom of God physical, emotional, and spiritual healing. The reason we do not see more angelic activity amongst the earthly armies of God is that they must be commissioned by us to be put into action. Most of us don't even realize angels have been assigned to us for that purpose, and lose out on the great benefit God has given to us as Christians. They will not move unless they are commanded to, and believe me, they are just waiting to hear orders from us so through the Spirit of God they can dominate the devil.

There are different types of angels in the heavenlies, and I will only take a brief time to mention them and their purpose.

1. Cherubim are angels who attend to God. (Hebrews 1:5-2:16)
2. Seraphim perform priestly duties. (Isaiah 6:1-7)
2. Archangels rule kingdoms and planets. (Colossians 1:15-18)
4. Michael is the chief prince of Israel. (Daniel 10:13, 21; 11:1; 12:1)
5. Gabriel stands before God and delivers important messages. (Daniel 8:16-19; 9:20-23)
6. Common angels are heavenly spirit beings. (Matthew 1:20-29; 2:13-19)
7. Guardian angels are given charge over us. (Psalm 91:12)
8. Ministering angels assist us in various ways. (1 Kings 19:5-7)
9. Avenging angels carry out God's judgment. (Genesis 19:1-29)
10. Death angels bring judgment. (Exodus 12:23; Revelation 6:8[6]

Ministering Angels

Of all the different types of angels at our disposal, I would like to focus our attention on ministering angels. Ministering angels assist our destiny. No one in the body of Christ achieves greatness without a lot of assistance. For everyone reading this book, you can admit that in your Christian life you have had help from various sources. We need mentoring more times than we are willing to admit. But without it, our purpose will never be accomplished.

> *Who has saved us and called us with a holy calling, not according to our works, but according to His own purpose and grace which was given to us in Christ Jesus before time began.*
>
> (2 Timothy 1:9)

The Greek word for purpose is *Pro thesis*.
Pro = before, to set before
Thesis = a written report[7]

Before you or I were born, God wrote our thesis and our purpose. That means God has created us to be victorious and will use any means possible to make that come to pass. That is where our angelic help comes from. In God's eyes, **IT'S ALL GOOD.**

An Angel Assigned to Gideon

When an angel was assigned to Gideon's life, he knew Gideon's destiny before Gideon did. There was an understanding of Gideon's assignment when the man of God did not have a clue. The angel knew of the great potential he possessed, and it was the angel's job to convince this fearful servant of God to own it. Potential means hidden, untapped, unfulfilled abilities. There is so much power and anointing God has placed inside of us that has been untapped, waiting for an opportunity to be unleashed. It is the job of angels to try to connect us to a time, an event, or a place that will unlock or unloose that potential. You and I are potent with destiny that is angel-assisted, guaranteed to be successful if we allow them to assist us in our lives.

Gideon was brimming with new confidence because of his encounter with God's angel. He was ridiculously confident that God would help Israel's army to come home victorious, so much so he only took 300 men into battle. When you realize they were going up against an army of about 135,000, it did not appear that victory was in their favor. When the dust settled that day, Israel had come home victorious after the Lord had confused the Midianites When hearing Israeli trumpets and the breaking of the jars they were holding it made the Israeli army appear greater than it really was causing the Midianites to run away in fear.

The Six-Day War

When we read accounts of the miraculous moves of God in the Old Testament, people are skeptical about the truth of the story. In their eyes, it is nothing more than a "fish story." This was the same reaction pretty much of people around the world when they heard of Israel's victory in the Six-Day War. In 1967, Egypt had been mobilizing its troops to destroy Israel. For much too long, the Israelis had been a thorn in the flesh to the Arab nations surrounding them. The leaders of Israel caught wind of rumors of an attack from Egypt. They decided to go on the offensive and strike first. Israel was hopelessly outnumbered: 465,000 Egyptian troops. Israel only had about 264,000 soldiers, over 200,000 of them being reservists. The battalion of tanks was also in Egypt's favor, numbering 2,880 compared to Israel's 800. The Royal Air Force of Egypt commanded 900 aircraft, when Israel could only muster up 300 airplanes.

Hopelessly outnumbered, Israel still believed they had the advantage because their God was on their side. On the first day when Israel struck, the Egyptians had no clue they were coming. It took Israel only twelve hours to pretty much destroy most of the aircraft available to their enemy. Unexplainable to Egyptian leaders, there was a malfunction of the anti-aircraft ammunition codes designed to destroy any aircraft entering Egyptian airspace. Even though Egypt was prepared to counterattack, airplanes never got off the ground and were destroyed by Israeli fighter planes. The destruction of Egypt's greatest asset in battle allowed Israelis to move to the next step in Israel's defense of their country.

In addition to the overwhelming fear by the Arabs, there are also many documented cases of large numbers of adversaries being inexplicably overtaken by just a few Jewish soldiers. In one such incident on the second day of the war, an enemy tank commander surrendered his obviously superior army to an Israeli force of 12 tanks. He later claimed that while only a few enemy tanks were present, a desert mirage made him see hundreds.[8]

Yisrael, Paratroopers sent to take the Tiran Straits recalls yet another incident. "The Israeli soldiers didn't have to parachute out of the airplanes. They landed like spoiled tourists in the airport, because the Egyptian Regiment which was on guard there fled before the Israelis were visible on the horizon. After landing, I was sent with another reserves soldier, *an electrician*, to patrol the area… (when) an Egyptian half-track appeared before us filled with soldiers and mounted with machine guns on every side. We had only light weapons with a few bullets that couldn't stop the half-track for a second. We couldn't turn back, so we stood there in despair, waited for the first shot, and for lack of a better idea, aimed our guns at them.

But the shots didn't come. The half-track came to a halt, and we decided to cautiously approach it. We found 18 armed soldiers inside sitting with guns in hand, with a petrified look on their faces. They looked at us with great fear as though begging for mercy. I shouted, "hands up!"... I asked the Egyptian Sgt. next to me, "Tell me, why didn't you shoot at us?" He answered, "I don't know. My arms froze-they became paralyzed. My whole body was paralyzed, and I don't know why.[9]

Although there is written testimony of the great miracles God had provided the Israelis to defeat their enemy in six short days, I would like to recount a testimony that I heard in a church service back in the early 70s. The preacher that day was of Arab descent and had a brother who fought in the Six-Day War. Much to the chagrin of the Arab nations, they could not explain how such a tiny, untrained army could dominate one of the finest armies in the entire world. To most Egyptians, this was the ultimate embarrassment.

One battle was never mentioned in the media, because if it had been, people would not have believed it anyway. This Arab preacher asked his brother what in the world happened, when Israel's demise was being reported before the actual event. The brother was fearful to divulge what the Egyptian army had seen, but when his brother would not take no for an answer, he told him this in these words: "We had backed the enemy up against the Red Sea. With the infantry closing in and the Navy in the Red Sea itself we were extremely confident in destroying their army that day. But... As we received the orders to fire, from out of nowhere giant angels with fiery swords came out of the desert where the Israelis were with the intentions of destroying us."

Now, anyone with half a brain would never believe an account like this. You would have to be insane to believe a fairytale so unbelievable as that. Look at what West Point officials admitted to when they were asked to explain what happened in the Six-Day War. "The US military Academy does not study the Six-Day War because what concerns West Point is strategy and tactics, not miracles."[10] Even the U.S. Army has to admit in certain cases, when a battle or war has been surprisingly won, there are no clear-cut military strategies that can explain such an anomaly.

Daniel Takes a Stand

In the Bible, Daniel took a stand for God when his "excellence" of life was rubbing his enemies the wrong way. His skill in his duties had exposed ineptness on their part, which in turn unleashed extreme resentment his way. It was their intention to knock him down a peg or two to level the playing field. This way they would not look so bad. These jealous leaders then set a trap they were sure would entangle Daniel, to be punished by death. A decree went out to punish anyone who prayed to a god other than the king himself.

Receiving news of the decree did not change Daniel's prayer habits. Three times a day he would open his window and boldly make his requests made known unto God. What led Daniel to be so defiant and confident that his God would protect him? A Scripture like this one could have been his inspiration to hold onto his faith.

Be strong and of good courage, do not fear nor be afraid of them; for the LORD *your God, He is the One who goes with you. He will not leave you nor forsake you.*
(Deuteronomy 31:6)

His personal relationship with the Lord was so dynamic, it took him to places that others could not find. Spending a long time in the presence of the Master made him privy to the secrets of heaven. That is how he found favor, although in captivity, with three different kings. When King Nebuchadnezzar was troubled by a dream he had and none of the king's men could interpret it, Daniel stepped to the plate and was able to answer when no one else could. When King Belshazzar succeeded Nebuchadnezzar, a hand appeared out of nowhere and began to write on the wall in a language that could not be understood. Again, Daniel headed to the palace to give an answer to the king. No one knows for sure what Daniel prayed before he was incarcerated, but it could have been something like this Psalm.

Hear the voice of my supplications when I cry to You, when I lift up my hands toward Your holy sanctuary.
(Psalm 28:2)

Time for an Angelic Intervention

It was time for an angelic intervention. His defiance of King Darius' order landed him in the lion's den, which was certainly a death sentence. But help came to Daniel from an unlikely source, the king himself. Darius was so distraught over having to put Daniel in the lion's den that he spent the better part of that night praying to Daniel's God. The message was immediately received and angels of protection were sent to the lion's den to make sure

Daniel would not be touched. The next morning, the king woke up early to see if his prayers had been answered. To his surprise, Daniel was not touched and gave glory to his God. The impact of this miracle is found in Darius' words in the book of Daniel 6:25-27.

> *Then King Darius wrote: To all peoples, nations, and languages that dwell in all the earth: Peace be multiplied to you. I make a decree that in every dominion of my kingdom men must tremble and fear before the God of Daniel. For He is the living God, and steadfast forever; His kingdom is the one which shall not be destroyed, and His dominion shall endure to the end. He delivers and rescues, and He works signs and wonders in heaven and on earth, who has delivered Daniel from the power of the lions.*

If you are faithful, God will always shut the mouths of your critics and your antagonists, and the enemies who try to destroy you will be few.

As inspirational as these testimonies have been, many have used the excuse that angelic help was for times past. Things have changed so much that we cannot be expected to unleash angelic power in the days we live in now. God has commissioned His Holy Spirit to bring the miraculous to this earth. I totally agree with that assumption, knowing that God's Spirit commissions angels to do His work.

Our experience with Angels

In 2016, we took a trip to Oregon, which would span for three weeks. As you all know, Oregon is in the northwest of the United States and is known for its cold, rainy weather. In October of that year, God had called us to that area. Our preaching tour had started off with a bang, in that for about ten hours, in three different services, the Lord was moving miraculously without reservation. If I am not mistaken, there were people healed from cancer and many other untreatable diseases.

Then the perfect storm hit my weakened body. The weather was cold, windy, and rainy. From the tiredness of my body, I could tell my resistance was very low and I got deathly sick. We went back to the mobile home we were using for our stay, asking the pastor if he would be so kind to bring us something to eat while we were trying to recuperate from such exhaustion. The flu-like symptoms, including a cough that lasted for our entire stay, knocked me out completely. After a week had passed, I was not feeling any better. At this time, the pastor recommended a doctor in the area who he was sure could help. The doctor checked me over and gave me some antibiotics, but he encouraged me to slow down.

I was scheduled to speak at least four times a week, and initially I thought I would just tough it out. But after the first week I had to cancel all my midweek services. Even on the second week, with a reduced schedule, I did not feel any better. While praying to rid myself of my physical problems, the Lord appeared slow in coming to my rescue.

My Understanding Was Opened

On the last day of our stay in Oregon, my understanding was opened. In fact, it came after the last service. It was a small congregation about thirty or forty in number. The Lord had moved graciously, but when a woman in the congregation came up to greet me after the service, she startled me with her initial statement. "I see angels." My eyes opened wide and I did not know how to respond. I guess with the amazed look on my face, she decided to explain what she meant.

"My prayer life has allowed me to be chosen by God to intercede in the behalf of His children to help them escape difficult times. When the Lord begins to speak to me in this fashion, I take out my drawing pad and draw the person or people God would want me to intercede for. He is very specific in getting the details of my assignment. He instructs me not only to draw a picture of the people I will be praying for, but details about them as well. When I saw you walking into the sanctuary this morning I freaked out. Up to this time in this ministry God has given me I never get to meet the people I am praying for."

I took the liberty to ask her to send a copy of what she was talking about. I almost fell out! On the next few pages, you will see in detail not only the drawing that has a good likeness to both me and my wife, but also specific details of us being evangelists, having a healing ministry, that we were driving in from the south to the north (which was true, from California to Oregon) and more. The most important detail of the drawing is our cry for help. It was then she began to intercede in her war tongues. I found out that because of her experience in the military, God has chosen her to transfer her military warfare tactics and use them for the kingdom of God.

What Guardian Angels Look Like

Now, most of us have not taken the time to understand the fact that our guardian angels look just like us.

So, when he had considered this, he came to the house of Mary, the mother of John whose surname was Mark, where many were gathered together praying. And as Peter knocked at the door of the gate, a girl named Rhoda came to answer. When she recognized Peter's voice, because of her gladness she did not open the gate, but ran in and announced that Peter stood before the gate. But they said to her, "You are beside yourself!" Yet she kept insisting that it was so. So they said, "It is his angel."

(Acts 12:12-15)

The early church was not startled by angelic visitation. It was a normal occurrence in their lives, knowing that ministering angels were sent to help in whichever way they could. The church of today has very little experience allowing angels to minister in that fashion.

I had never ever seen or heard of a ministry like this woman had described. My mind began to rewind the last three weeks, and all the bickering and complaining to God I had done, I finally came to the realization that He had my back all along, sending angels to speak to a woman who had a powerful intercessory prayer ministry. All I could do was weep and plead for forgiveness, for which I felt undeserving.

08 Jan 2016 @ 2:48am
Stroke/heart attack victim
gets bad headaches/migrains
issue with hands?

Gifts of Spirit?

Grey/white balding

Age 60-70s
weight 175-190
5'10-6'

light skin but has foreign accent

Keeps repeating "Pray for me! Pray for us!" Not sure who "we" or "us" are has "halo" ora, so is Holy Ghost filled & baptized in Jesus Name. May be a preacher - teacher - evangilist @ one time.

By Invitation Only

- January 08, 2016 @ 2:48 am
- Stroke / heart attack victim
- Gets bad headaches / migraines
- Issue with hands?
- Gifts of Spirit?
- Grey / white balding
- Age 60-70
- Wight 175-190
- 5'10" – 6'
- Light skin
- But has foreign accent
- Keeps repeating "Pray for me! Pray for us."
- Not sure who "we or "us" are
- Has "halo" ora, so is Hoy Ghost filled & baptized in Jesus Name
- Maybe a preacher – teacher- evangelist at one time

09 Jan 2016 @ 08:32am
Says "Pray for me! Pray for us" but I don't know who she is talking about. No names are being given.

She only lets me see side view/¾
Pacing
halo = A.G.
Filled
Baptized in Jesus name

dark or black hair
darker skin
accent. maybe Cuban or Mexican South American
Influenza?
Stomach/intestinal issue?

Age: 50-60s   125-155   5'4-5'6

"I am his wife" = Who's wife?
"Not dead"? Why am I seeing her if she is alive still? Traveling? Sick?

Compass. Shows her in a car w/ male figure heading North from the Southern state. "I-5" sigh ½ Mt. Shasta shown. Who do I know that speaks Spanish CA state going to WA or OR?

By Invitation Only

- January 09, 2016 @ 08:32am
- Says "Pray for me! Pray for us"
- But I don't know who she is talking about
- No names are being given
- She only lets me see side view / & Pacing
- Halo = H.G. filled
- Baptized in Jesus name
- Dark or black hair
- Darker skin
- Accent maybe Cuban or Mexican, South American
- Influenza?
- Stomach / Intestinal issue?
- Age 50 -60s
- 125 -155
- 5'4" -5'6"
- "I am his wife" = Who's wife?
- "Not dead"?
- Why am I seeing her if she is alive still?
- Traveling? Sick?
-
- Compass shows her in a car w/ male figure
- Heading North from the Southern state.
- Shown "I-5" Sign & Mt. Shasta
- Who do I know that speaks Spanish?
- In CA state going to WA or OR?

Most Christians are Unaware of Angelic Help

Let me say this as plain as I can. Most Christians today are unaware of angelic assistance in their lives. In their eyes, what is more real are the cartoonlike depictions of angels. They truly are a disservice to the mighty ministry God has given to them. It is an embarrassment to believe that many people view angels as Cupid-like figures. Let me give you a more realistic view of the angels that are assigned to us. We find that angels are mighty and powerful (Revelation 18:1). Unmistakable, angels are patient and meek (Numbers 22, Jude 9). Though they are invisible, at times they can be seen (2 Kings 6:1). Angels watch us and listen to our words (1 Corinthians 4:9). They help in time of danger, deliver from distraction, and destroy if the need arises (Joshua 5:13-14, Daniel 10:4-14). Angels receive their instructions from God and are under His authority (1 Chronicles 21:15).

You would think that God in His infinite wisdom would have commanded angels to take care of us here on earth whether we liked it or not. But in reality, angels are commissioned into our lives much the same way God moves in us. Unless an invitation is made, no matter how threatening a situation could be, both God and angels show up by invitation only. Yet, there is a promise that all of us should take into consideration and take advantage of. We find that promise in the book of Psalms.

> *The angel of the LORD encamps all around those who fear Him, and delivers them.*
>
> (Psalm 34:7)

A Powerful Promise

What a powerful promise that encourages us to know that at any time, anywhere, our guardian angels are out 24/7 with no need for sleep. I believe Elisha the prophet understood this promise more than most of God's children today. He so exuded confidence in his walk with God that in turbulent times he did not waver in his faith in God, and that faith gave him an unfair advantage when dealing with his enemies. His cool, calm, and collected demeanor was so impressive it appeared he did not sweat. This was how he responded to a situation that had freaked out his servant. Perhaps hundreds of soldiers were ready to cross over to take them both prisoners back to the king. This was Elisha's response to all the hoopla.

> *So he answered, "Do not fear, for those who are with us are more than those who are with them." And Elisha prayed, and said, "LORD, I pray, open his eyes that he may see." Then the LORD opened the eyes of the young man, and he saw. And behold, the mountain was full of horses and chariots of fire all around Elisha.*
>
> (2 Kings 6:16-17)

Who do you believe these men actually were? Angels, of course. Angel armies, ready to be put into action at the sound of His voice. These angels assigned to you are just waiting to hear that same command so they could gladly respond, "AT YOUR SERVICE."

The man or woman who is wholly and joyously surrendered to Christ can't make a wrong choice any choice will be the right one.

A.W. Tozer

Chapter 5

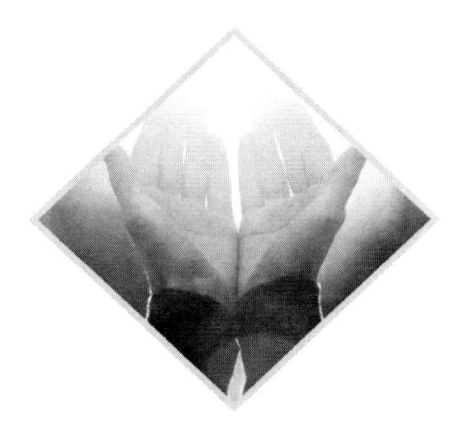

IF AND ONLY IF

Except when there may be no poor among you; for the LORD will greatly bless you in the land which the LORD your God is giving you to possess as an inheritance — only if you carefully obey the voice of the LORD your God, to observe with care all these commandments which I command you today.

(Deuteronomy 15:4-5)

In all the books I've written to date, there is at least one chapter that does not follow the theme of the book.

You have now come to that chapter. In actuality, this chapter is an extension of material I wrote about in my last book (See "Not Afraid of the Deep"). It is so important a subject that a continuation explaining the concept is necessary. We will revisit the subject of presumption, because it is presumption that has been confused for faith. We also know if faith is not at the foundation of our beliefs, our walk with God will be deficient.

My First Experience with "IF Statements"

Back in junior high school, I was required to take geometry in my studies. Math had never really been a strong point in my educational pursuits and having to spend a year learning and memorizing different theorems made matters worse. So, some forty-odd years later, things have not changed a bit. But as much as I hated my math class, never in my wildest imagination did I believe the learning of "if statements" would benefit me in my spiritual life. If statements are used to help prove theorems. Without going into great detail, I will try to simplify the concept as best I can. "If statements" are always conditional, meaning if a hypothesis is true then it will cause the conclusion to be true. If more than one condition is not met, the statement cannot be true or come to pass. Now, let's go back to the Bible and put it into biblical terms.

Example: If you pray, then God will answer your prayer. There is Scripture to back that statement up:

> ...*The effective, fervent prayer of a righteous man avails much.*
>
> (James 5:16)

Call onto me, and I will answer thee...
(Jeremiah 33:3 KJV)

These two scriptures are true, so the assumption is made that God answers all prayer.

But what about Psalm 66:18 and Isaiah 1:15

If I regard iniquity in my heart, the Lord will not hear.

When you spread out your hands, I will hide My eyes from you; even though you make many prayers, I will not hear. Your hands are full of blood.

When we add the last two Scriptures, it puts a stop to the "name it and claim it" doctrine and stops presumptuous errors in their tracks. We can then use these if → then statement rules to help us avoid egregious errors in our attempt to understand the word of God. There were times in my early days of serving God that I would try to find shortcuts to obtain the answers I wanted from Him. I would casually search the Scriptures and if I could find one or two verses that would back up my petition, then I would use those scriptures as a crutch to wait for my answer. I can't tell you how many times that way of thinking eventually failed to bring me the result I was looking for.

Presumption is Not Faith

The subject of presumption is one of the most misunderstood concepts of the Bible that has stunted the growth of Christians for generations. The misapplication of presumption, believing it to be faith, has caused many a heartbreak. Presumptuous faith is not of God because it is reckless, and I can even go as far as calling it diabolical. It is out of control, irresponsible, and initiated from hell, not from God. Jeremiah states that our heart is desperately wicked and who can know it? (Jeremiah 17:9) If our desires are not God-initiated, He has no responsibility to give us what we ask. You might say, "I can't really believe what you are writing because it goes against Scripture and what I have been taught all my life." Let me find a Scripture to help prove my point.

> *Ask, and it will be given to you; seek, and you will find; knock, and it will be opened to you. For everyone who asks receives, and he who seeks finds, and to him who knocks it will be opened.*
>
> (Matthew 7:7-8)

If God has not initiated the desire in your heart, He has no obligation to bring it to pass. The scenario I will mention is so common amongst us, that at one time or another all of us have gone down this path, and when getting to the end without receiving what we have asked for, there is confusion. You can take one Scripture and magically create a doctrine. Scriptures go together to help us avoid atrocious errors that may have been committed in the past. Let me give just one Scripture among many that would disprove our belief that God will give us whatever we ask.

> *Surely God will not listen to empty talk, nor will the Almighty regard it.*
>
> (Job 35:13)

I've known people in the past who misunderstood "faith" Scriptures, using them and God gave them what they had asked and it caused a lot of grief.

"If Statements" Protect Us

"If statements" become our protection in that they spell out exactly what must be done to receive from God. The instructions given are precise, and although challenging at times, they are very doable. They must be followed exactly as requested, and if so, God will release His blessing. Anything less will negate the promise. Let's go back to Scripture.

If you are willing and obedient, you shall eat the good of the land.

(Isaiah 1:19)

There are two, not one, conditions in this passage of Scripture for the promise to unfold in our lives. One or the other not applied breaks God's promise. The example given in Matthew 21:28-30 bears this out.

But what do you think? A man had two sons, and he came to the first and said, 'Son, go, work today in my vineyard.' He answered and said, 'I will not,' but afterward he regretted it and went. Then he came to the second and said likewise. And he answered and said, 'I go, sir,' but he did not go.

As you can see, the first son initially said no to the command of his father. He later changed his mind and did go. On the other hand, the second one initially accepted his father's order but then eventually did not. The second son was willing but not obedient, whereas the first one eventually became willing and obedient complying to his father's wishes.

Only One Salvation Plan

We can apply this to the Christian world as well. When the Lord initiated the salvation plan, there was one and only one way to comply. In the days in which we live, we have so many different religions because we pretty much pick and choose what to believe or not. The word of God was written to be obeyed from cover to cover, knowing that God does not change with time or seasons. People are being saved by obeying Acts 16:31, which says:

So they said, "Believe on the Lord Jesus Christ, and you will be saved..."

Folks who are saved under those conditions have the first part right, and there is a willingness to make a change in their lives. What they seemed to overlook was the obedience part. Repentance alone does not save anyone, it's just the first step in the process. Look how Luke describes it again in the book of Acts 2:38:

Then Peter said to them, "Repent, and let every one of you be baptized in the name of Jesus Christ for the remission of sins; and you shall receive the gift of the Holy Spirit.

How important is the repentance part in the cycle of receiving salvation from above? That question can be answered again in God's word:

...But unless you repent you will all likewise perish.
(Luke 13:3)

Once the initial steps are taken and obeyed, heavenly power is released to help the born again Christian to evangelize a lost world.

Abraham's Dilemma

Abraham found himself in a dilemma that weighed heavy on his conscience. His nephew Lot found himself in grave danger because of the lack of spiritual maturity in his life. Fed up with the sinful lives of those living in Sodom and Gomorrah, the Lord had decided to destroy everyone inside the cities. The concern Abraham had for his nephew was more than Lot deserved. He was a two-faced believer in his service to God. When it was convenient for him to do the work of the Lord, he was all in. He appeared to relish the respect his position in the city allowed him. Because he was more out than in, those living inside of Sodom never knew he was a man of God. At the same time, he had allowed worldly concepts and thinking to pollute his faith. The lines of clarity between the holy and unholy became more blurred, to the point where he eventually couldn't tell the difference. This came to light when he offered his daughters to the men of the city who were trying to convince Lot to release the new men (i.e., angels) they had seen come into his home. They of course had only one thing in mind and that was to sexually abuse them. Hoping to appease them, Lot offered them his daughters instead. What kind of father would do that? Lot did not have a clue as to believing he had done anything wrong. Lot was willing to, on one hand, bring safety to his heavenly visitors, but on the other hand he was also willing to forfeit the virginity and well-being of his precious daughters.

But Abraham in his spirit felt uneasy and began to pray for his wayward nephew. Not knowing for sure what was going on in the life of Lot, he began to pound the throne of God with his intercession.

The far-reaching love God demonstrated for Lot was unbelievable. Abraham knew he needed to take matters into his own hands to remedy this situation, so he not only prayed, he PRAYED! His intercession was incredible in that he was able to negotiate an escape for Lot when the Lord had already decided all in the city were going to be destroyed. Let me make one thing clear, negotiating with God is possible when you have taken the time to get to know Him as He really is.

II Chronicles 7:14 - The Five "Ifs"

When new concepts are being presented, caution is exercised before we go head over heels to believe something that we are not used to. Let me present to you another "IF" to help you stabilize your thinking in this new concept. In reading 2 Chronicles 7:14, if we observe closely we will find five "IFs" in this passage of Scripture.

> *If My people who are called by My name will humble themselves, and pray and seek My face, and turn from their wicked ways, then I will hear from heaven, and will forgive their sin and heal their land.*

I think most oneness Pentecostals don't understand the power given to them by being called by His name (Jesus). Every promise and blessing hangs its hat on the name of Jesus. Without it, it's just religion. His name must be applied to our lives if our salvation is going to be true.

Nor is there salvation in any other, for there is no other name under heaven given among men by which we must be saved.

(Acts 4:12)

The second "IF" is the phrase, "will humble themselves." I have found in my ministry while dealing with sick folk, most of them who ask for prayer are not physically hurting. Their pain comes from either an emotional problem from their past or spiritual problems that have not been resolved. The key to each and every healing is their ability to humble themselves and admit what the Word of Knowledge has shown me through the Holy Ghost. If they are honest with me -- and believe me, people do lie to the ministry -- they will leave the church that night completely healed. That is how powerful humility is. That's why Peter wrote in his epistle:

Therefore humble yourselves under the mighty hand of God, that He may exalt you in due time

(1 Peter 5:6)

Taking the High Road

I cannot count how many times I have asked people to take the high road and ask an offended family member for forgiveness even when the other party was at fault. There is one case in particular I would like to share. There was a young man with problems causing severe pain in his groin. When I told him in secret why it happened, he almost fell out.

I said more or less in these words, "You have had a bitter disagreement with your mother. Although you did not initiate the problem, the Lord is asking you to take the first step in asking her for forgiveness."

He responded in this way: "I would if I could, but I have lost track of her, don't know where she lives, and the phone number I have is disconnected."

I then told him this: "If you are willing to do what I have asked, I will pray for you and in three days you will receive a phone call from your mother." He didn't know whether I was kidding or just out of my mind.

Well, long story short, a couple of weeks later I received a phone call from him, declaring he had patched things up with his mother when just like I prophesied he received a phone call from her. To make the blessing even more powerful, he was completely healed.

"Pray with supplication." Asking the Lord in humility, as I have mentioned, is powerful, but even more so when your prayer is a prayer of supplication. I read somewhere a definition of supplication that I would like to share. Supplication is asking God in all honesty, as children talking to their kindhearted father, but ending with "Your will be done." That is one of the best words of advice on praying I have ever read.

Seeking God's Face

"Seek God's face." Most children of God are not "seekers." We use that word loosely, but truthfully, we are more like "lookers." Looking for God has the feel of a casual search for something or someone, not really knowing what you are trying to find. A search, on the other hand, is more intense. When a child has been kidnapped or somehow disappears, the authorities don't send out a looking out party. They will call on their best searchers to find that child. Because of their experience, they know how to search and where to search, doing it in the shortest period of time, knowing that time is of the essence. A child of God having an attitude of a searcher is one who brings delight to the heart of God. His search for God becomes more of an all-out assault on His kingdom. It's a no holds barred fight to the finish, and like Jacob, you don't let go until God blesses you. It is aggressive, and yet at the same time it is passionate.

> *I call to remembrance my song in the night; I meditate within my heart, and my spirit makes diligent search.*
> (Psalm 77:6)

The final "IF" in 2 Chronicles 7:14 is, "Turn from our wicked ways." There are folks who have been saved long enough to have allowed sins committed before conversion to come back into their lives. Because they have learned how to play the game, they believe it is no longer necessary to hold such a tight grip on their salvation. In their eyes, it's time to loosen the belt because face it, they are a lot better than what they used to be. The reminder is there, and it is just as important to heed and keep this warning as it is to comply with all the rest.

When all five conditions, nothing less, are placed into practice, the promises of this Scripture will come to pass. God then will hear from heaven, resulting from a clear connection and no distortion. He can then forgive all sin, which in His eyes includes forgetting. The last promise of the Scripture will then take effect, healing the land. This extends to the wilderness, fields, countryside and all the inhabitants of the whole entire world. If and only if you are willing to do it God's way.

Obedient to an Unfair Request

Several years ago, I dealt with a married couple who were struggling in their marriage. In actuality, the wife was going through the needless suffering because the husband was closed-minded to her needs. To add more stress to her life, a child was born to them with physical problems. She initially came up front to have me pray for the baby, but I was able to discern the reason why the baby could not walk, and it was not physical. When I have to dig into the secrets of others' lives with a Word of Knowledge God has given me for the situation, I ALWAYS will share the results with that person in secret. No one else could hear what I was telling her as I whispered in her ear something like this: "Take the brunt of the problem in your marriage and don't talk back, put it in the hands of the Lord and God will take care of it."

Initially, she felt I was being unfair, and like other marriages receiving counsel, taking the side of the husband. I know what she was feeling because in my own life there have been times the Lord had asked the same of me. Especially when you don't understand the why of it all, humbling yourself is never easy. In my life, for years there was a disconnect between a family member and me. When the Lord asked me to take the initiative and make things right, I was apprehensive, thinking it was not fair. I then came to the conclusion it was worth the trouble if this problem could be resolved through my humility. As the Lord placed this wife in a similar situation, she reasoned, what did she have to lose? If this was the key for her baby being healed, it would be worth the sacrifice. I then prayed for her and we waited on God.

I had forgotten about this situation, when about three weeks later or so on Facebook, I received a picture of a baby walking. It was sent from the pastor I had ministered for about that time. The photo was taken in church and the entire congregation was rejoicing, because that day the little girl who could not walk started walking again. For all the suffering the mother endured, she could not compare it to the joy she was now feeling. Her baby is now walking without any problems and to see her, you would never know she had suffered in that manner.

In the kingdom of God, the Lord never asks us to do the impossible. Why? That's because the impossible is His job to fulfill. The key to receiving our blessings is promised through His word in an "if statement."

If you are willing and obedient, you shall eat the good of the land.

(Isaiah 1:19)

If I should write of the heavy burdens of a godly preacher, which he must carry and endure, and I know from my own experience, I would scare every man from the office of preaching.

Martin Luther

Chapter 6

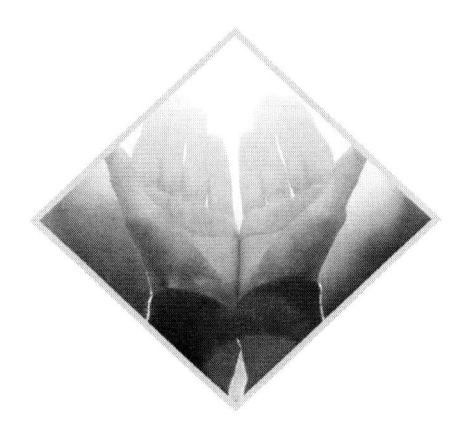

INCONVENIENCED

Very truly I tell you, when you were younger you dressed yourself and went where you wanted; but when you are old you will stretch out your hands, and someone else will dress you and lead you where you do not want to go."
(John 21:18-NIV)

Being inconvenienced is something personal in that some things bother some people and for others it's not a problem. Being inconvenienced means a trouble or difficulty interfering with one's personal requirements of comfort.[11] Let me illustrate with an example that happened when I was first married. We lived in a beautiful apartment complex, but one of our neighbors was truly a neighbor from hell. He had a short fuse and was very finicky about his privacy. We lived on the second floor just above his apartment, and believe you me, "everything" bothered him. Let me elaborate.

The Neighbor from Hell

We had no central air-conditioning and we all know second floor apartments are always much hotter. We used a box fan in our bedroom to cool us off, but the vibration of the fan, which was normal, irritated him. Any time he disagreed with something we were doing, he would start banging his broom on his ceiling to make us stop. Another time while playing the piano, that again was discomforting to him, so he would bang away again until we stopped. My wife could not even walk through the apartments in heels because it was a no-no as well.

One day he was so angry that he ran up the stairs and started banging on the door like a madman., scaring us half to death. I hurried to open the door and he chewed me out something fierce. What a temper he had, which was scary because he was a Highway Patrol officer. We had visions of him coming upstairs locked and loaded, then blowing us away. Needless to say we did not stay in that apartment very long. That, my friend, is what I call being inconvenienced. Me more so than him.

Inconveniences come in all sizes, shapes, and forms. It can be the most insignificant thing to the most unnerving. Whether big or small, the result is still the same in that you are left feeling uncomfortable. It is very difficult to gauge a person's tolerance level because we are all unique, and what does not bother you can actually irk someone completely, to react to you irrationally. Knowing that this is a fact of life, we as Christians must understand God uses these unfortunate occurrences to build our character.

It's Going to Hurt

Now no chastening seems to be joyful for the present, but painful; nevertheless, afterward it yields the peaceable fruit of righteousness to those who have been trained by it.
(Hebrews 12:11)

The word chastening has been misunderstood for generations. It was taught to me over forty years ago to mean punishment. If you read the Bible in Spanish, it actually does translate that way. But chastening is a type of training and character building, not punishment. It is a grueling process that can cause extreme discomfort, mental anguish, unbearable physical pain, and can go on for an extended period of time. I have mentioned this in other books I've written, but it bears repeating. Back in my high school days when I played football, we as the players, 100% agreed that the coaches were trying to kill us. In their experience, they knew this type of training was necessary because we would face teams in our schedule that would be bigger, faster, and at times more experienced. Our ability to outlast them physically, playing at an uncontrollable pace, paid dividends when in the fourth quarter they always wilted under our constant pressure. At season's end, we then understood and appreciated the hard work we put in to become champions. That being said, going through this type of training is very slow, arduous, and backbreaking.

The Lessons We Have Learned from Peter

As we examine the life of the apostle Peter, there are so many lessons we can learn from this man of God. Before he knew the Lord, he was quite a character and continued to be so after his conversion. The Gospels are full of his experiences and his name comes up second only to that of Jesus. No disciple spoke so often and so much as Peter, he was incredible in this facet. When Jesus took the time to speak to His disciples, He spoke more to Peter than all the rest. His character was flawed and needed to be adjusted. He was also more presumptuous than any other disciple, yet he took it upon himself to reprove the Lord (Matthew 16:22). At the same time, no other disciple ever so boldly confessed that Jesus was the Christ. What made Peter so complicated was at the same time he could intrude, interfere, and tempt Him like none other. There were times Jesus spoke words of approval, praise, and blessing. Then at the same time He could say harder things to Peter than He could to any of the other disciples.[12] If Peter was going to be successful in the kingdom of God, he would have to be completely broken and reformed into the image of Christ.

> *And whoever falls on this stone will be broken; but on whomever it falls, it will grind him to powder."*
> (Matthew 21:44)

No one comes to the kingdom of God without having adjustments made to their lives. Whatever walk of life a person has lived will never fully prepare him for the life he will now live. You have entered into a place where "normal" is somewhat bizarre. If need be, time and experience are pushed aside and do not carry the same weight that they did previously, in life as we live it right now. You are now in God's kingdom, playing by His rules, and He is in complete control of everything.

In the case of Peter, he was indirectly told this when Christ renamed him Cephas (the man of rock). The renaming was prophetic in nature because that was how the rest of the world would see this gung-ho disciple. At the time of his calling, he was unstable, but God would mold him with a strong, firm hand.

Peter's Molding Begins

When the molding began, Peter's life oozed with potential and the possibilities of success were endless. The Lord took advantage of his experiences in sea life and consequently used examples that he would be familiar with. To get to that point, the Lord would have to deal with his resistance to pressure and it took three different calls on Peter's life to have him get on board. Being hardheaded did not help the situation, nevertheless, the Lord knew how to get His man. The first call from God was for Peter to believe (Matthew 4:18). The second call found Peter following Christ casually (Luke 5:3). The final call was more direct and it was a call to have no other master (Luke 5:11).

His first training session we find in Luke 5:4-5, dealing in an area of expertise for Peter.

> *When He had stopped speaking, He said to Simon, "Launch out into the deep and let down your nets for a catch." But Simon answered and said to Him, "Master, we have toiled all night and caught nothing; nevertheless at Your word I will let down the net."*

Peter was being inconvenienced by a man who knew nothing about fishing. "Nevertheless or in spite of what I think, at your word, I will let down the net." It is somewhat difficult to actually recreate Peter's voice, whether he actually in humility let down the net or it was said mockingly. Whichever way it did come out, the result was the same. Jesus produced a miracle, whether He knew anything about fishing or not. This would not be the last time Peter was humbled by obeying the Master.[13]

Another Sea Episode

Another sea episode that became part of Peter's training occurred when a need to pay taxes showed up. On this occasion, the Lord would kill two birds with one stone. Not only would He show the disciples the importance of obeying the laws of the land, but also produce an unexpected miracle at the same time. It would come from Peter's obedience to a really bizarre order from the Lord. Peter was told to once again go fishing. How Peter received his assignment, we are not really sure, but talk about inconveniences. Was he expected to catch the number of fish needed to pay the tax all by himself? It probably wasn't the best time to expect a great catch, but the Lord was trying to break Peter of his old ways of thinking to prepare him for bigger and greater things.

> *Nevertheless, lest we offend them, go to the sea, cast in a hook, and take the fish that comes up first. And when you have opened its mouth, you will find a piece of money; take that and give it to them for Me and you.*
>
> (Matthew 17:27)

Still, there is yet another sea adventure the Lord used to train Peter. On this occasion, the Lord used a storm as a classroom to increase the faith of His servant. Storms were not really new to Peter, because as a fisherman he encountered many a storm in his experiences. By this time he was fearless and bold, knowing how to deal with any type of storm that would come his way. But this storm was not an ordinary storm, and it had Peter inconvenienced. When it appeared this storm would overtake the ship, he along with the rest angrily awakened the Master, who was sleeping peacefully. "Do you not care that we perish?" they questioned in unison. Because of his presumptuous nature, I can only imagine Peter was the loudest in his complaint. His past experiences dealing with storms told him that unless something out of the ordinary happened, they were going to die. What I like most about how Jesus handled the problem was that He did not even respond to their question. This is what He did.

> *Then He arose and rebuked the wind, and said to the sea, "Peace, be still!" And the wind ceased and there was a great calm. But He said to them, "Why are you so fearful? How is it that you have no faith?" And they feared exceedingly, and said to one another, "Who can this be, that even the wind and the sea obey Him!"*
>
> (Mark 4:39-41)

Chalk another one up for the Lord, because I am sure this was another experience in Peter's life that left him with his mouth open.

The Training Continues

The Lord continued His personal training of His disciples, and in particular Peter, with this next sea experience. On this occasion, as the disciples left on a boat crossing the Sea of Galilee, something unconventional was added to their experiences with Christ. The Lord had stayed behind to pray. Stop the testimony a moment to make this important observation. If Jesus, the ruler of the universe and Savior of our souls chose to pray here on earth, how much more should we follow His example? Let the Scripture tell the story:

> *Now in the fourth watch of the night Jesus went to them, walking on the sea. And when the disciples saw Him walking on the sea, they were troubled, saying, "It is a ghost!" And they cried out for fear. But immediately Jesus spoke to them, saying, "Be of good cheer! It is I; do not be afraid." And Peter answered Him and said, "Lord, if it is You, command me to come to You on the water." So He said, "Come." And when Peter had come down out of the boat, he walked on the water to go to Jesus. But when he saw that the wind was boisterous, he was afraid; and beginning to sink he cried out, saying, "Lord, save me!" And immediately Jesus stretched out His hand and caught him, and said to him, "O you of little faith, why did you doubt?" And when they got into the boat, the wind ceased.*
> (Matthew 14:25-32).

Taking your eyes off of Jesus will always bring inconveniences to your life. What was the last thing Jesus wanted Peter to learn? Don't look at your circumstances, keep your head up and your eyes on Jesus, and He will provide the answer you need.

One last observation before we move on. The raging storm stopped only after Jesus and Peter got into the boat, but Peter was saved from the moment he placed himself in the arms of God. Your raging storm may not have ceased in your life as of yet, but be assured, being held in the arms of God is the safest and best place you could be.

One Last Sea Episode

There is one last sea episode I would like to mention. This particular event happened after the resurrection of Christ. Probably Peter is yet traumatized over the brutal death of Jesus, feeling somewhat responsible in that he himself could not stand up for the Lord when Jesus needed him most. He had always found comfort and peace in fishing and believed that that would be the solution to getting on with his life. He understood he had done his best, and yet his best was not good enough. Whether he verbalized his thoughts or not, he was able to convince the other disciples to join him again in the fishing business. In this particular occurrence their efforts had been in vain, in that they were not able to catch a single fish. They had decided to give it up when they heard a familiar voice:

> *And He said to them, "Cast the net on the right side of the boat, and you will find some." So they cast, and now they were not able to draw it in because of the multitude of fish.*
> (John 21:6)

With the enormity of the catch, it finally dawned on Peter that the one making the suggestion was the Lord Himself. What at the outset appeared an inconvenience, turned out to be another opportunity to allow God to show His miraculous self.

Dealing with Peter's Heart

Taking advantage of the situation, the Lord decided to deal directly with Peter's heart. He knew that Peter's inborn confidence in himself turned him into an idle boaster, throwing caution to the wind at every opportunity to make himself look good. He uttered magnificent promises, which he afterwards shamefully broke, and was always cleaning up his messes after creating disasters. This is yet another example where Peter goes to "cleanup on aisle 4."

The Lord has a tendency to ask questions He already knows the answers to, but asks them anyway. He was about to go into the probing mode by asking Peter a question three different times, in different ways as well. The first dagger into the heart came when Jesus addressed Peter by his original name; i.e., Simon, as if he had forfeited the name of Peter through his denial of Christ. Talk about being inconvenienced. Then the Master asked the million-dollar question, "Lovest thou me more than these?" This was an easy yes or no question, but Peter put the responsibility for the answer back in the Lord's hands by saying, "Yea Lord; thou knowest that I love thee." We must not be surprised to have our sincerity called into question, when we ourselves have done something that makes it doubtful. His triple confession succeeded his triple denial, and that was enough for Christ.[14]

Peter Now Understands His Mission

Peter now understood his mission, which would be beneficial to him for the rest of his life. The Master died to self before He died for sin. Any child of God used in His kingdom successfully has taken the same pathway. It was then that Peter would follow in Christ's footsteps.

For to this you were called, because Christ also suffered for us, leaving us an example, that you should follow His steps: "Who committed no sin, nor was deceit found in His mouth"; who, when He was reviled, did not revile in return; when He suffered, He did not threaten, but committed Himself to Him who judges righteously.

(1 Peter 2:21, 23)

One of the greatest lessons Peter had learned was that inconveniences would not deter him in his service to Christ. It was to become the new normal in his life so he would not be distracted from his destiny.

Peter's Final Request

After preaching on the day of Pentecost when a great revival broke out, the molding of his character continued to his death. Every once in a while, glimpses of his past would sprout up; i.e., the brashness shown in the day of Pentecost message. He would stumble every so often, most notably the prejudices towards Gentiles when he was surrounded by Jewish leaders. Paul had to put him in his place, and I'm sure for Peter it was quite embarrassing. But, as time went on, Peter's maturity began to blossom and it really came to the forefront at the time of his death. Tradition says (because there is no Scripture to confirm) that Peter's death came by crucifixion. Again, tradition states that Peter had one last request before dying for the cause of Christ. He asked to be crucified upside down because he was unworthy to die in the same manner as his Savior. I can just about hear him saying, "If it's not too much of an inconvenience, please honor my request."
With his pride now in check, he would die in peace because God's grace would be sufficient to take him home.

> ..."*God resists the proud, but gives grace to the humble.*"
> (1 Peter 5:5)

I would like to close this chapter by revisiting the Scripture we initially posted.

> *Very truly I tell you, when you were younger you dressed yourself and went where you wanted; but when you are old you will stretch out your hands, and someone else will dress you and lead you where you do not want to go.*
> (John 21:18-NIV)

Identifying with Peter's Life

At the time of the writing of this book, I am about to turn sixty-three years of age. I can't actually say that the experiences I am now having are much different than what I had to struggle with throughout my entire life. Physically speaking, my life has ALWAYS been a challenge. Without rehashing, what I have written in my other books, most of you know that from the age of five I have had to deal with the effects of suffering from polio. Because of God's grace, I have lived a pretty normal life, in my eyes anyway. But as I draw closer to the mid-sixties, I identify so much with the Scripture above. After suffering a heart attack and stroke in 2013, I no longer drive because of a neglect in my eyesight. Consequently, someone has to drive me everywhere I go, usually my wife. Because of a freak accident, the toe on my left foot had to be amputated. That has limited my ability to enjoy outdoor sports, especially jogging, which was one of my passions. Doctors have recently told me the shrinking of muscles on my right leg cannot be fixed medically because they do not have a clue as to what is wrong. I have been prayed for, but as of yet the physical confirmation has not presented itself. Little by little, I am losing more strength and mobility in my hands. That being said, on bad days I cannot dress myself. Finally, my doctor says that my kidneys are close to being put on dialysis, which will restrict my freedom even more. O how I identify with the apostle Peter in his sufferings, yet I am not discouraged.

Inconveniences: Just a Part of Life

For those of you who believe I am sharing this for your pity, think again. These inconveniences are a part of living in an imperfect world. If all I had to look forward to was what I experience here on earth, I would be utterly depressed. But, until I am not able to lay hands on the sick, allowing God to heal them, I will not allow the inconveniences of life to destroy me. I will fight to the bitter end!

We travel an appointed way.

A. W. Tozer

Chapter 7

A GODLY SORROW

He was despised and rejected by men, a Man of sorrows and pain and acquainted with grief; and like One from whom men hide their faces He was despised, and we did not appreciate His worth or esteem Him.

(Isaiah 53:3 AMP)

We use revisionist history more than we are willing to admit. Although by definition, revisionist history is a reinterpretation of orthodox views on historical events[15], we use it also in our everyday lives. Have you ever heard of "fish stories? Fish stories are ones where the event or situation being described becomes larger than life as time goes on. Case in point. A very nonathletic young man brags about the number of letters he has won in various sports in high school, and he has his letterman's jacket to prove it. The truth is those letters were won as a manager for each team, not as an actual player. There is no one to refute his claim, so his statement remains impressive and his self-esteem skyrockets.

Biblical Revisionist History

As bad as that sounds, what is even worse is when biblical truths of the past have been revised to fit the interpretation of the days in which we live. Over the years, many truths have been revised and at times replaced to be non-offensive to those who are seeking a watered-down, more convenient religion. The greatest issue I have with these revisions is that truth does not need revising.

> *Do not remove the ancient landmark which your fathers have set.*
>
> (Proverbs 22:28)

Making changes for change's sake will lead you down a slippery slope. Because much of our beliefs rely on faith, changing them because they do not make any sense to us only weakens our relationship with Him.

Erroneous Views of Christ

Let us take a look at some erroneous views of Christ that in some eyes are truth. There are no photographs from the time of Christ to verify what He looked like, but artists' renditions of today paint Him with long, flowing, frilly hair, with rosy cheeks. In line with that depiction,

A Godly Sorrow

Jesus is portrayed as a soft-spoken person with an endearing voice. He is gentle in every way, unassuming, and would not kill a fly. Jesus is also depicted as a man who was emotionally detached, meaning He could never have a bad day because He was always in control. We desire to be like Him because He never backed down from a challenge. What is most impressive to me was the belief that Jesus was always successful when He prayed. He was in such control of His emotions that nothing ever bothered Him in that manner. That is how revisionist history paints the picture of our Savior.

Now for the truth! The Scriptures tell a different story. The crucifixion disfigured Him beyond recognition.

Just as there were many who were appalled at him -- his appearance was so disfigured beyond that of any human being and his form marred beyond human likeness.
(Isaiah 52:14 NIV)

There were times He hid himself from danger.

Then they took up stones to throw at Him; but Jesus hid Himself and went out of the temple, going through the midst of them, and so passed by.
(John 8:59)

Believe it or not, there were times Jesus could not heal the sick.

Now He could do no mighty work there, except that He lay His hands on a few sick people and healed them.
(Mark 6:5)

Emotionally distraught, He wept over Jerusalem.

> *Now as He drew near, He saw the city and wept over it…*
> (Luke 19:41)

Revising the Scriptures

As time has gone on, many have revised the Scriptures to their liking, many times modifying His law to the law of the present time. Nothing is sacred anymore and all is held to the interpretation of the day. Yet, there is a strong admonition from heaven to the children of God to keep His word and His commandments.

> *Jesus answered and said to him, "If anyone loves Me, he will keep My word; and My Father will love him, and We will come to him and make Our home with him.*
> (John 14:23)

Going back to revisionist history, it would be easy to believe the acceptance of Christ's ministry was worldwide because of the great multitudes of people He drew. Again, the Scriptures paint a different picture.

> *…He was despised and rejected by men…*
> (Isaiah 53:3)

What does it mean to be despised? By definition, it is the feeling that a person or thing is beneath consideration, worthless, or deserving scorn.[16] The opposition He encountered was relentless. They would laugh and deride Him to no end. If this had not been prophesied, then perhaps it would have been unbearable.

A Godly Sorrow

This is the word which the LORD has spoken concerning Him: ...the daughter of Zion, has despised you, laughed you to scorn; the daughter of Jerusalem Has shaken her head behind your back!

(Isaiah 37:22)

A loose translation from the Hebrew tells us that He was unworthy of attention. The Pharisees, Sadducees, and Romans had it in for Him. To this day, the contempt amongst the Jews for Jesus is as strong, if not more so, than at the time He lived on this earth. Because He was an unattractive man, nothing like He is depicted today, it made it easier to dislike Him. People tend to hover over good-looking folks, and from Scripture Jesus was not pleasing to the eyes. It has always been human nature to give a break to good-looking people with great personalities, and dressed well to boot. Jesus did not fit that picture.

...He had no beauty or majesty to attract us to him, nothing in his appearance that we should desire him.

(Isaiah 53:2 NIV)

Did Abuses Affect Him?

Most people believe because Jesus was not only a man but God as well, criticisms or abuses ongoing until His death, did not affect Him. He was not a robot, heartless in any way, but flesh and blood with emotions just like you and me.

But I am a worm, and no man; a reproach of men, and despised by the people.

(Psalm 22:6)

You cannot be plainer in describing His self-esteem. His words demonstrated just how deep the criticism for Him would really cut. This was a prophecy that would help us to understand just how emotionally attached Jesus was to this dying world. Nevertheless, He dealt with it and did not let it hinder His purpose in giving His life for humanity.

He was rejected because of His beliefs. He was so radical in the eyes of the Jews that they had steam coming out of their ears in disgust. They could not believe He had the audacity to break the laws of the Sabbath day, even if it meant bypassing a sick man in need of healing. With these words, He put them in their place:

And He said to them, "The Sabbath was made for man, and not man for the Sabbath. Therefore the Son of Man is also Lord of the Sabbath."

(Mark 2:27-28)

He was rejected because He didn't fit the part. They could not see Him as having a significance for them, so consequently they wanted no part of Him.

He was in the world, and the world was made through Him, and the world did not know Him. He came to His own, and His own did not receive Him.

(John 1:10-11).

He projected a life in disarray with so many unsolved problems. How could He bring a nation out of captivity when He could not take care of Himself? He was a vagabond of sorts, not to speak of His followers, who were nothing more than misfits. Jesus did not fit the mold of what a Messiah was supposed to look like, much less act like. The Jews were completely caught off guard and were not prepared to deal with a man who did not look like a king.

He Did Not Act Like a King

The presence or demeanor of a king exudes confidence, trust and inspiration. Jesus was so far removed in those areas that His appearance caused the opposite reaction. Yes, He made an indelible mark, but it was not what you think. Suffice it to say He was a Man of Sorrows, and this would define Him. It was the unlikely power He would use to draw all men unto Him. It was quite the opposite of what we look for in a leader, right? Actually, the "Man of Sorrows" moniker He would carry was the charm He would use to keep men near Him. Not His cheerfulness, not a pleasantness of speech, but His sorrowful nature.[17] He wore "sorrow" as medals of honor, just like a proud soldier serving his country.

His life was one continued series of sorrows, from the cradle to the grave.[18] As a baby, his parents fled from Herod to escape death. As a child, He was full of thoughts that could not be uttered. Can you imagine the frustration of a child not being able to verbalize his thoughts to help people in need? That was His life, and He had to deal with it in silence. As a man, He was misunderstood and reviled. What helped Him was the fact that many of the sorrows were sorrows for others. He sorrowed over bodily suffering, which He encountered pretty much every day. The despair He found in those who had been turned away from the medical profession, broke His heart. He could not avoid the sorrows He expressed over the mentally ill, for they above all were being neglected because society had no use for them. What brought the greatest of sorrows was the compassion. Because compassion indicates the ability to contain something felt for the lost. That is the single reason He left heaven: to bring salvation to a lost world.

Only a Man of Sorrows Could Save the World

Only a man of sorrows could be the Savior of the world. The nature of sorrow itself brings a man closer to the truth and causes him to make sacrifices he would not normally make. Sorrow can make a man more useful, not to mention more sympathetic to those living in sorrow as well.[19] One of the reasons I believe the healing ministry God has given me has been so successful is because of the sympathy and empathy I have for those I minister to. It is not a stretch to place myself in their shoes, because I have not only been there in the past, but even to this day deal with such issues.

You would think that doing good and producing miracles would cause people to receive God with open arms. But, because Jesus' miracles were done on the Sabbath, the Jews could not get past their tradition even though they were breaking it in one way or another themselves. No wonder His reaction to them was one of disgust.

> *And when He had looked around at them with anger, being grieved by the hardness of their hearts, He said to the man, "Stretch out your hand." And he stretched it out, and his hand was restored as whole as the other.*
>
> (Mark 3:5)

Grief Was His Middle Name

He was acquainted with grief. In other words, He was known by His grief. Sorrow and grief were His constant companions and His life was one continued series of sorrow. He was exceedingly sorrowful in the garden, demonstrated by His sweat that appeared as blood. One can only imagine the guilt of the sins of humanity that weighed so, so heavily on His heart. Death on the cross was not only painful, but bearing the agony of the shame was overwhelming. Remember, being crucified was considered a curse, a total embarrassment not only to the one being crucified, but also to the family.

> *"If a man has committed a sin deserving of death, and he is put to death, and you hang him on a tree, his body shall not remain overnight on the tree, but you shall surely bury him that day, so that you do not defile the land which the LORD your God is giving you as an inheritance; for he who is hanged is accursed of God.*
>
> (Deuteronomy 21:22-23)

These sorrows were an uninterrupted succession of suffering, which He was willing to bear. In that hour, Jesus rejoiced in spirit and was given proof that through His sacrifice, Satan would finally be defeated. It was at this time Jesus had forgotten the load of His grief. He beheld Himself through His sacrifice, exalted as a conqueror. The prophecy was finally coming to pass as death loomed near.

> *He shall see of the travail of his soul, and shall be satisfied.*
>
> (Isaiah 53:11)

Nothing He could say or do would lessen the pain and suffering Golgotha's hill would create, nevertheless, His knowledge of prophecy allowed Him to endure to the end, knowing it would be worth it all!

They Hid Their Faces from Him

You would think that the arrival of the promised Messiah would have caused such a great stir and excitement amongst every Hebrew who was anticipating His coming. Again, Scripture tells us the contrary. Isaiah 53:3 tells us that His people hid their faces from Him. They were so afraid to associate with this man from Galilee because His ways, methods, and teachings were too bizarre. Although He would heal the sick, putting spit and/or mud on blinded eyes was not what they were used to seeing. In reality, they had never seen anyone heal the sick in their entire lifetime like He did. They probably could have gotten used to His unique methods of healing the sick, but when He was constantly breaking the laws of the Sabbath by healing people on that day, it was just unacceptable. I can imagine the stir that was made when He was found alone with a woman in public. A true man of God would not disrespect the law in the fashion He had. Of Isaiah 53:3, one translation puts it this way: He was as one who hid his face before us, alluding to the Mosaic law.[20]

> *And the leper in whom the plague is, his clothes shall be rent, and his head bare, and he shall put a covering upon his upper lip, and shall cry, unclean, unclean.*
>
> (Leviticus 13:45 KJV)

They Could Not Accept His Ministry

His acceptance into the Hebrew community was rejected because His manner of ministry and way of life was as damning as a life of a leper. Whichever way He turned, somebody was always gawking. He was such an object of contempt because He had caught them completely off-guard and was nothing like what they had expected the Messiah to be. So, they hid their faces and turned away in scorn.

If hiding their faces was not enough, they continued showing their displeasure in Him by not esteeming Him. It has been my experience, in serving the Lord, that there are quite a few people who typically disregard others who suffer in the Lord. For whatever reasons, good or bad, the sufferers are not accepted in the inner circles of certain churches. It is almost a way to continue despising and rejecting God Himself, because they really don't believe it's God's will for His children to be suffering. In their estimation, it is a lack of faith on the sufferer's part, and they need to repent. That being said, the people of Israel could not esteem Him, so instead they disrespected Him in such a vulgar manner. They scorned Him, and had a disregard for His authority. They were genuinely rude and were not fearful to demonstrate their insolence to Him. It is very similar what we here in the United States are experiencing with the negative reaction to our new president. Because it was such a shock that he actually won over the front runner from the other party, the reaction to his winning the presidency is infantile. I am not really heavily involved in politics, I am only stating an observation.

What the Jews should have given Jesus was their respect, their esteem, total recognition, and humbly glorified His name. They were so entrenched in their hatred for Him, they could not figure out what they had lost in rejecting this man of God. The promised Messiah was right before their eyes, but He slipped through the cracks because their loathing blinded them to the truth.

The Scriptural Account Has Been Ignored

Revisionist history has diluted what really happened at Calvary. Many believers were shocked when the movie, "The Passion of the Christ" made its debut. From what I heard, many people who had seen the film felt that the graphic portrayal of the beating of Christ was not only barbaric and unrealistic, but completely over the top. Many critics have complained that the producer and writers went to an extreme using their historical license, and consequently distorted the truth. In the days in which we live, it is not politically correct to believe that was an actual occurrence, yet it did happen exactly the way Isaiah wrote it. The Jewish nation was up in arms and grossly offended by the fact the blame for Christ's brutal death was placed on them.

The truth of the matter is that Christ's death was brutal. It was most definitely brutal. Put your revisionist history aside for a moment and look how Isaiah prophesied over the death of Jesus.

> *Just as there were many who were appalled at him -- his appearance was so disfigured beyond that of any human being and his form marred beyond human likeness.*
>
> (Isaiah 52:14 NIV)

There it is, in black and white. There is no holding back on the brutality the Scriptures depict. How badly must a man be beaten for one to be appalled at his appearance? How bruised must he have been to be unrecognizable to those who knew him? At the end of the beating, one could not even tell if it were human or not. Remember, those are not my words, that is Scripture.

A Godly Sorrow

Why Was It All Necessary?

Was this all necessary to buy back salvation for all of humanity? He did it with no guarantees that we would accept His sacrificial offering to bring that salvation to our lives. Don't let His death be in vain.

But as many as received Him, to them He gave the right to become children of God, to those who believe in His name.
(John 1:12)

It took a man of sorrows who took the world by storm to redeem it back to Him. Now it's time for you to GIVE YOURSELF AWAY to Him.

There is a time when we must firmly choose the course we will follow, or the relentless drift of events will make the decision.

Herbert V. Prochnow

Chapter 8

PHYSICIAN, HEAL THYSELF

He said to them, "You will surely say this proverb to Me, 'Physician, heal yourself! Whatever we have heard done in Capernaum, do also here in Your country.'"
(Luke 4:23)

Going back home is not always a positive experience. I say that because for the person who has left, chances are great changes have been made and you are no longer the same person. As those people try to re-associate themselves with you, they find the way you live now is so different than what they had remembered. They might see a lot more good, but then on the other hand, they see a part of you that blows them completely out of the water. Depending on the changes themselves, many will like the new you. Others will not respond so positively because now you appear so much better than they are, educationally, financially, not to mention socially, and it's somewhat difficult to handle. The skeptical ones at times appear to be those you were closest to, but they just don't know how to handle the new you.

When I Returned Home

I have had that experience myself. When I left my local church where I was saved and ministered for a little over thirteen years, I was much more reserved and timid than I am now. I ran the Christian school but only preached once a month. When I had returned after being away for several years those, who knew me had to do a double-take when I began to move in the realm of the miraculous. It was like, "Where in the world did all that come from? We never saw any of that while you were here, what gives?" I had the same response from them that Jesus had when He returned to Nazareth and could do no miracles. In my case, upon my return visit, they realized that after leaving them, I continued to grow It was somewhat disheartening to admit they were pretty much in the same place as they were when I left.

Jesus Causes an Uproar

…*"Assuredly, I say to you, no prophet is accepted in his own country.*

(Luke 4:24)

In the case of the Messiah returning to His place of upbringing, the reaction of the townsfolk was even worse. When He stood up that day in the synagogue and declared what Luke wrote to us in chapter 4 verse 18, the scandal and uproar caused by His words would not be settled so easily.

The Spirit of the LORD *is upon Me, because He has anointed Me to preach the gospel to the poor; He has sent Me to heal the brokenhearted, to proclaim liberty to the captives and recovery of sight to the blind, To set at liberty those who are oppressed.*

(Luke 4:18)

These words left the crowd completely bewildered, walking around somewhat astonished at the gracious words coming out of His mouth. Yes, they were witnesses, but no, they did not believe it.

So all bore witness to Him, and marveled at the gracious words which proceeded out of His mouth. And they said, "Is this not Joseph's son?"

(Luke 4:22)

To them, it did not make any sense. In their eyes this was all a hoax, which made them so angry they rose up, and took Him out of the city to kill Him, but He escaped out of their grasp.

Now He did not do many mighty works there because of their unbelief.

(Matthew 13:58)

The assignment given Jesus, to convince the Jews He was the Messiah, would be an uphill battle if there ever was one. He needed to prove that He was the one they had long been waiting for. That was a tall order because they were expecting a royal, powerful Messiah, something of course that He was not. If Israel were to come out of captivity, their leader would also have to be a great warrior. His battle savvy would inspire so many to fight gallantly, Israel would never lose another war. So, His healing touch had to be dynamic and out of the ordinary to capture their attention, because if not, then His work here on earth would be in vain.

The Master's Touch

Knowing His healing power went beyond the physical realm, it touched humanity in every deficient area of their lives. His touch was compassionate and identified Him with suffering people. It also broke down walls of alienation and prejudice. He touched the untouchable to prove a point -- anyone could receive healing if they only asked. These people Jesus was dealing with needed proof He was who He said He was. In the past, they had heard similar rhetoric, but kingdoms are not taken over by words, and this time they would not be so easily convinced. They flat out said it in plain words, "If you are the Messiah, prove it by performing glorious miracles.[21] If Capernaum could brag about the miracles you performed for them, surely you could do the same in your hometown." Somehow, I believe the challenge made to the Lord was not so they could marvel at His ability to perform miracles. I believe they wanted Him to make the attempt so that in failure they could mock Him. And of course, it had to be done in the middle of their city to make it legitimate. The phrase, "physician, heal yourself," is like the American proverb, "charity begins at home."[22] More specifically, doctors should practice their medicine at home. This was the bottom line: show us signs and wonders and we will believe you. They were going to make sure He would prove it.

Jesus Responding to Opposition

Their audacity to Him and His ministry raised His ire, and He responded to them very harshly.

> *But I tell you truly, many widows were in Israel in the days of Elijah, when the heaven was shut up three years and six months, and there was a great famine throughout all the land; but to none of them was Elijah sent except to Zarephath, in the region of Sidon, to a woman who was a widow. And many lepers were in Israel in the time of Elisha the prophet, and none of them was cleansed except Naaman the Syrian." So all those in the synagogue, when they heard these things, were filled with wrath,*
>
> (Luke 4:25-28)

The Lord's rant was so incendiary, it caused the crowd that day, filled with wrath, to lead Him onto the brow of the hill where the city was built that they might cast Him down. But because it was not yet time for Jesus to die, He was able to escape to live another day.

Jesus needed to see their participation in receiving their own healing and the healing of others. Faith was a necessary ingredient, and once it was released on their part, then Jesus would perform the miracles they were looking for. I can identify with the Lord in this case, in that when I am ministering at the altar, dealing with the sick, many people I encounter want me to jump through hoops and perform miracles that would leave them in awe. You should see the look on many faces when I tell them in secret, for them to receive their miracle that day, they would have to first repent of a sin or bad habit that was hindering their healing. There are those who have angrily stomped off to their seats, muttering under their breath that that was never going to happen. Consequently, they are still battling with the same physical issues that brought them to the altar in the first place.

How I Got Involved in Ministry

Now, I would like to tell my story as to how I got involved in a healing ministry. Although from my childhood there was a great desire to be used by God in this manner, as I took inventory of the gifts I had or mostly did not have, I came to the conclusion that being used of God in this manner was out of the question. I was not only ill-equipped to be successful, but my fears that I wouldn't be good at it dominated my thinking. One of the major reasons I was hesitant to accept this new challenge was because I was not fluent in the Spanish language. Being a member of a Spanish organization where 95% or so of the congregations spoke only Spanish, I knew I would have my work cut out for me. If the language would have been my only obstacle my apprehension to begin ministering in Spanish would not have been so great. But because I am a "Pocho - an American-born Mexican" the rift between Mexican nationals and Mexican-Americans is similar to the one between Jews and Arabs. As much as I tried to get out of my assignment, the Lord was very stern in His position of leading me in this direction. The nationals were brutal with me and that they would literally laugh as I was ministering and it made me feel so uncomfortable. I had to learn to take it, because once they were able to see how I was used in the miraculous, they had to back down pretty much from their ridicule. Because I humbled myself and continued to peck away at becoming proficient, little by little the laughter died down to almost nothing.

The burning desire I had to be used by God overrode the deficiencies I had to perform the work set before me. The Lord in His wisdom knew He could make up the difference through His Spirit for me to have any kind of success. So, I placed myself wholly and totally in the hands of God, and it was enough to start me on my way. I found out later the reason why signs, wonders, and miracles suddenly became a normal part of my ministry. It had nothing to do with begging or pleading with God. Initially in my walk with God, all I ever wanted to be was pleasing to Him. Spending time alone in His presence became my passion. There were occasions in the presence of God that I literally got lost in Him, not to mention losing track of time. I don't know how many years my approach to God in this manner continued, but if these experiences with Him were going to be the pinnacle of my experience with the Lord, I would then die a happy man. But, without even asking the gifts of the Spirit began to flow freely, and initially it really frightened me. I could not believe a man like me, quiet in nature, could be used successfully in a Pentecostal atmosphere.

A Great Lesson of Grace

It was here that I learned a great lesson of the grace of God. I say that because with all the success I have had, in retrospect it had to be God leading, guiding, and anointing me to perform the miracles through His Spirit. I am amazed how people overlook my physical deficiencies to allow God to do the impossible in their lives. It was then that my wife and I began to travel internationally, but the greatest surprise God laid on me was the ability to put my thoughts in writing to become an author. To this day, I have written ten books (five in both Spanish and English). The one you are reading at this moment is number six. Looking back at this time in ministry, I finally felt that I had turned the corner when something unexpected turned my life upside down.

2013 Brings Unforeseen Challenges

An unseen challenge arose in 2013. In October of that year, I suffered a stroke and a heart attack. Because I have mentioned this in my last book, I will not go into great detail here. It took several months to recover, and the only lingering defect of the whole ordeal is that the stroke has caused a neglect in my right eye. My peripheral vision has been taken away, and consequently I no longer drive. There are quite a few other physical concerns and challenges I have at this present time that I would like to mention. My right leg is shrinking and losing muscle mass and strength. The neurologists we have seen have admitted to us they are dumbfounded by this occurrence and cannot suggest any type of remedy and/or therapy to strengthen my leg. Whether the polio has returned to my body or not, they cannot say, but the only thing they are sure of is that they cannot help me at this time. Not only has the leg begun to shrink, but I have begun to walk with a limp, more like weeble-wobbling. Added to my physical challenges are my weakening kidneys. My nephrologist (kidney doctor) says my kidneys are functioning at only 25%, and if the percentage goes any lower he is thinking to put me on dialysis. As concerning as that sounds, there is something that may be less threatening, but in my view more troublesome to deal with. That has to do with how I am dealing with the big toe on my left foot being amputated. The amputation is making it more difficult to exercise and walk as well.

So why is that so important? In the past, I have used exercise to spend extra time in prayer with the Master. It has also been very therapeutic for me to go outside and appreciate everything God has created. I have spent many a time meditating and getting lost in His presence while I was jogging, but for now it has been limited to walking.

What I don't Want God to Heal

There is one last physical issue I would like to mention, but it is one that I will never ask God to heal. It has to do with the aftereffects of my suffering with polio. For those of you who do not know me, polio affected my upper body, most notably on my right side. My arms and hands are weakened, so consequently I will use my mouth to do things I normally do with my hands (opening jar lids, opening plastic baggies, unscrewing bottles etc.). It has gotten worse since my left thumb has started to lose strength. Why wouldn't you want God to heal you completely when it would bring to Him such honor and glory?

If God were to heal me and make me normal like everyone else, it would be difficult to remember the miracles He performed when He miraculously healed me of polio at the age of five. Like Jacob after a life-changing encounter with God, he left that encounter limping for the rest of his life. I am sure that every time someone asked Jacob what had happened to cause the limp, he had the greatest answer anyone could give. It allowed him to share his once-in-a-lifetime battle, going toe to toe with the Lord and coming out on the winning side. It was how he was able to get God to change his name from Jacob to Israel. The only drawback of this great victory was that he would have to spend the rest of his life walking with a limp. I too have put up with well-meaning people trying to help me understand that my handicap could be healed by the Lord. And although I have suffered some criticism, if not bewildered stares, I am willing to put up with the inconvenienced this misunderstanding brought into my life. (See Chapter 6 --Inconveniences)

Physician, Heal Thyself

I have taken the time to write about the Lord's struggles in getting Israel to understand why He was sent into this world. Now I would like to take His words, "Physician, heal thyself," and apply them to my life. I have painstakingly jotted down the physical issues I am now battling. Some of those can only be healed by a touch from God. But, it is the ones that I have control over that I would like to discuss. When the Lord initially placed the title of this chapter in my mind, it was also a wake-up call to my dwindling physical condition. He has instructed me to take the reins of these illnesses and do something about them myself. Consequently, my wife and I are on a mission to rid ourselves of our problems with diabetes, high blood pressure, and high cholesterol, doing it holistically. We are in the process of reevaluating the way we eat, our exercise habits, and have started to make the necessary changes to bring complete health back into our lives.

In making this decision, the Lord guided us to a holistic doctor who is Spirit-filled. He is amazing in that his entire office every Friday closes at midday. What's so amazing about this? The entire staff stays until regular closing hours, spending the time interceding for the people they have attended to. The spiritual attacks on his office are real, in that on more than one occasion witches have snuck into the office, praying their incantations to destroy the work being done by these Christian doctors. He was so moved by my poor health that when I saw him for the second time, he told me this: "George, you are my new assignment. The Lord has instructed me to care for you at no charge and I am to do this until you are well." I was floored, and at the same time felt special in that the Lord would speak to a doctor unknown to me to make sure I would be restored to health.

An Experience I Will Never Forget

Through my holistic doctor Ted Edwards, I was referred to a Spirit-filled minister and his wife who do counseling. In our session, as we got into the Spirit, a message was given to me from the Lord. It said:

You will accomplish your purpose! You will accomplish your purpose! No, your life will not be cut short, I have greater plans for you.

You will provide an inheritance; it will be above and beyond what you could even imagine. You are not worse than an infidel. You are my precious child of God!

Ride it out and finish the course. It's a narrow and distinct road. I have appointed you a time to die and nothing will get in the way of that!

I Give Myself Away

You will pass on to the next generation all that I have given to you to spread to the entire world the gifting that I have given you.

Jesus
January 5, 2017

    As I rewrite this message, the tears are streaming down my cheeks. I can still feel the emotion and love God demonstrated to me that day when He graciously gave me this message. I had been stressing over my future much because my health was quickly deteriorating. Because of circumstances beyond my control, I was not yet ready to end my life, because I needed to make sure I would leave for my children an inheritance that would be useful in their lives after I was gone. After receiving this message, I was completely humbled and yet encouraged that the Lord does have great plans for me. What have I done to deserve such love from a God who is ever so gracious? Is it any wonder why I am willing to GIVE MYSELF AWAY to Him?

    At the end of this chapter I had intended to leave a diary of a thirty-day detox program we found to bring us back to health. It is very rigid, so much so, that after starting it for two weeks, the program was too intense for my body and it kind of went into shock. We were able to find another program just as effective without the body becoming so stressed. I backed off a little bit and eased into another program, this one written by a Christian woman, with much more success. At the time of publishing, I have lost 27 pounds, 6 inches on my waist, and my blood sugar is averaging in the 130s. I am slowly but surely weaning myself off of my medication. With God's help I will be off my meds completely in about 30 more days. If you are interested in using the same program, it is called:

The Shepherd's Diet
Kristina Wilds

PHYSICIAN, HEAL THYSELF

All our dreams can come true, if we have the courage to pursue them.

Walt Disney

Chapter 9

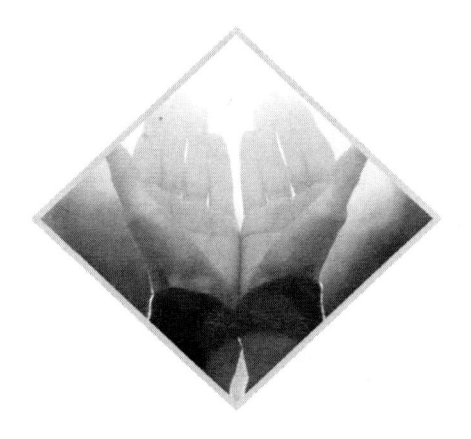

IT'S NEVER TOO LATE

"The harvest is past, the summer is ended, and we are not saved!"

(Jeremiah 8:20)

Old Testament farmers in Palestine knew exactly how much time was needed for a successful harvest. Harvesting was done three times a year, followed by a feast. Passover[23] is the feast celebrated in the spring, commemorating the liberation of the Israelites from the Egyptians. Pentecost[24] commemorates God's giving of the Ten Commandments at Mount Sinai, forty-nine days after the Exodus. The last of the sacred holidays is called the Feast of Tabernacles.[25] While crossing the Sinai desert, the Jews built temporary shelters to house themselves. This celebration commemorates that with the building of sukkah (booths), and for seven days living in them, so their descendants would remember the suffering Israel endured before the Lord brought them out. This last week marked the end of the calendar year.

The climate during the harvest (April-September) is hot, dry, with little or no rain. The climate tends to be stable and very rarely varies from the norm. The importance of rain during the planting season is paramount in that without it the crops would wither and die. Because Palestine isn't known for its large rivers, it was absolutely essential for starting and maturing crops. The rains falling on Israel were very consistent in that one could count on a former rain and a latter rain to fall every year.

Israel's Spiritual Drought

Spiritually speaking, Israel was in a drought as well. Their sin had brought judgments upon them and consequently they found themselves in captivity. They were in a state of hopelessness, with no remedy in sight. What the Scripture above is trying to tell us is that Israel had been alienated, done away with, overrun, and God was provoked to anger. They had been consumed, destroyed utterly, made to feel like a waste. If there was ever a picture of despair, this was it!

There were certain laws of the harvest needing to be considered.

1. Gleaning of the harvest was prohibited.
2. A person could not reap a harvest without actually working in the field.
3. All blessings were earned and the first fruits were given to the Lord.

The repercussions sin has on mankind are always the same. You can change the time period, the place, the situations, but sin will always rear its ugly head to take what it wants. The greatest consequence and/or ramification of sin is that it will always separate us from His presence. After Adam had sinned in the garden, he hid from God because for the first time in his entire life he understood he was naked. His sin also caused the glory of God to vanish from his life and consequently brought with it fear for the first time.

...I was afraid because I was naked; and I hid myself."
(Genesis 3:10)

Over the years, sin continues to make us feel naked before Him and somewhat defensive. I know exactly when my children have done something wrong because their pride goes up and immediately they become defensive. Not knowing whether I know the truth about what is going on or not, their guilt has ratted them out, with nowhere to hide.

The Lord asked Cain a simple question (Where is your brother?) and look how guilty he sounded in response to it.

..."I do not know, am I my brother's keeper?"
(Genesis 4:9)

Shifting the Blame

Sin will cause us to make excuses, bringing to the forefront our insecurities. Putting down someone to make yourself look better is a sign of immaturity, a trait no one can afford. Both Adam and his wife, Eve fell into the same trap. They tried as hard as they could to avoid accepting responsibility, and in return put the blame on someone else. When the Lord was trying to get to the bottom of the situation, Adam was the first to step forward and shift the blame to his wife.

The woman whom thou gavest to be with me...IT'S ALL HER FAULT. (Genesis 3:12)

Eve, on the other hand, would not be outdone with her response to the Lord. as well. The serpent beguiled me...IT'S ALL HIS FAULT

If we are not willing to take responsibility for our actions, then guilt will alienate us even more, to the point we feel there is no remedy to our situation. It is Satan's mission to utterly destroy us. Look how the apostle John so clearly makes this point in John 10:10:

The thief does not come except to steal, and to kill, and to destroy...

Mercy is not in his vocabulary, and understand, he will be relentless in the pursuit of our soul. That does not intimidate our God one bit, because in the same breath, the same Scripture, the Lord fires back with a death blow the enemy is unable to recover from, ...*I have come that they may have life, and that they may have it more abundantly.*

How can we be sure He can reach us? Like the Jews, sin has taken its toll on us and like them, we've been alienated, got away with, overrun, consumed, destroyed utterly, and we feel like waste. The Jews were honest when they described their despair in Jeremiah chapter 8. *"The harvest is passed, Summer is ended."* In other words, our time for salvation has passed us and there is no way around it. It was so easy for them to sulk in their misery, forgetting how powerful God's love and forgiveness were for them. All they had to do was go back to nature and see how God took care of His creations. The rain came after every summer, no matter how dry the land had gotten. It was always enough to produce a harvest that would bring blessing to God's people. No matter how hot, dry, or miserable the summer had been, God would make it right with a latter rain and then sealing the deal with a magnificent rainbow.

The Latter Rain Today

How does that affect us, you might ask? He will also use the "latter rain" to renew us when we have fallen down, fallen apart, and just hopelessly fallen. In the Old Testament, the Scriptures help us to understand that this outpouring of rain was considered a special blessing.

> *And it shall come to pass in the last days, says God, that I will pour out of My Spirit on all flesh; Your sons and your daughters shall prophesy, Your young men shall see visions, Your old men shall dream dreams.*
>
> (Acts 2:17)

The outpouring of the Holy Ghost was the greatest spiritual rain experienced by mankind. It continues to be the catalyst the Lord uses to grow His Church in this last hour and will do so until the time of His second coming. It goes without question that this generation of believers has embraced the gifts of the Spirit like never before. On any given Sunday, it has become customary to see prophesying in church services as something to be expected. It is also becoming more frequent not only hearing of young men receiving visions from God, but the older generation are receiving their messages from the Lord in the form of dreams as well. This outpouring of God's Spirit goes hand-in-hand with another Scripture with promise.

> *But you shall receive power when the Holy Spirit has come upon you; and you shall be witnesses to Me in Jerusalem, and in all Judea and Samaria, and to the end of the earth."*
> (Acts 1:8)

Embellishing Our Role Today

Again, the Church of today has embellished their role as Holy Ghost-filled crusaders, taking the gospel throughout the world. The old phrase, "Our four and no more," has been kicked to the curb, being replaced by a generation on fire, screaming, "Our four and millions more." They are out to do serious damage to Hell's kingdom, and they are not letting anything get in their way. They have heavily armed themselves with the gifts of the Spirit flowing mightily in their everyday lives. Signs, wonders, and miracles have broken out in droves and are being used by this younger generation to duplicate something the first church was known for. They are turning the world upside down and Satan cannot stop it.

But, what does that say to the individual who has spent all of his life ignoring the Master's call? He has chosen to live his life apart from God, never taking into consideration the salvation that has been offered freely. He has squandered his opportunities to use whatever gifting God has mercifully given him, and in reality is not even aware of the enormous impact in the Christian world he could have if he only surrendered his life to the Lord. He wanders aimlessly, never finding his purpose in life, and consequently fritters away his time in projects that have no eternal value. If and when at the time of his death he has an opportunity to make things right with God, in many cases the guilt stockpiled in his heart is so great that a "last second" acceptance of God is considered hypocritical.

Our Family Experience

I would now like to share an experience in our family that recently happened (July 2016). My wife comes from a big family, a total of nine brothers and sisters. It is a close-knit family, as most Hispanic families are, and the bond they share is a firm one which was cemented when a decision was made to leave Mexico for the United States. My wife Maria, being one of the younger children, was cared for by her older siblings as her parents went back and forth, bringing children into the country one at a time. Her older brother, Pepe and her sister, Hermila were basically the ones who kept an eye out for her as they all acclimated themselves to living in a new country. The bond continued to grow, and for many years Sundays were spent relaxing in the park, playing sports, eating good food, and just enjoying a good time of fellowship with each other. Their faith of choice was Catholicism, but it was more by tradition than belief.

Some years passed, and something happened that would become a chink in the armor of their relationship. My mother-in-law, sister-in-law, Pati, and my wife converted to the Oneness message and were baptized in Jesus' name, becoming Christians. Of course, as excited as they were with their newfound faith, it only seemed natural to share this new way of life with the rest of the family. It brought a strain in their relationship, because leaving Catholicism for Christianity was, in their eyes, an act of betrayal, and they really didn't want to hear about it.

The great show of love God demonstrates in our lives is beyond comprehension, and His willingness to wait until we are ready to look His way is astounding. The repercussions of a lost opportunity to spend eternity with God cannot so easily be pushed aside, and yet it happens all the time.

Years had passed and we were not making any headway in convincing the family to follow us in forming a personal relationship with God. As far as they were concerned, they were born Catholic and they would die Catholic. Then tragedy struck in the form of CANCER. My brother-in-law, Pepe had gone to the emergency room, suffering from excruciating headaches. In examining him, doctors found tumors growing at a rapid rate and decided to immediately operate to see if they could catch it before any other damage could be done. We were told that the cancer was infecting his kidney and spreading to his brain and lungs. Because kidney cancer is an aggressive cancer, there was great concern amongst all of us.

Knowing that he was not a religious man of any sort, his condition affected us (my wife and I, her mom and sister) differently, in that the rest of the family was more concerned over his physical condition, when we were concentrating more on the spiritual side. If we could reach him spiritually, helping him understand the deficiency in his relationship with God and convince him to give his life to Christ, even if he were to die, at least we knew heaven would be his eternal home. Our attempt to get him to open up to the gospel initially fell on deaf ears. But the sicker he got, the more open he became to listen to what his mom and sisters had been trying to communicate to him for years.

A Change of Heart

He continued to weaken and the situation did not look very promising. In the interim, almost every day my mother-in-law and sister-in-law, Pati would visit him in the hospital, reading the Bible to him, and singing the beautiful Spanish hymns that began to grip his heart. You could start to see a change in his countenance, and for the first time there was an initial desire to learn more about Jesus. When Pati and my mother-in-law continued to unfold Scriptures of repentance and salvation, the light turned on, and for the first time he began to understand what it was to form a relationship with God. He had a sudden hunger to pray and communicate with his Creator, but not knowing exactly how brought great frustration to him. The times my sister-in-law and mother-in-law spent singing praises unto the Lord were finally hitting home, and with tears in his eyes he made a decision to be baptized in water, turning over his life to the Lord Jesus Christ, a decision he would never regret.

Satan Fights Harder

It is somewhat incomprehensible to understand the extremes Satan goes to, to gain the life of a lost soul. Nothing is too dirty or underhanded for him to back away from an opportunity to take just one more. The fight we then encountered was fierce, because just about everywhere we turned, the doors of opportunity to get him baptized in water were being shut. The hospital would not give permission for him to be baptized there because in their eyes the liability was too great. Pepe's wife and sons would not permit him to go home and do the baptism for fear he would die there, and they did not want to deal with that kind of memory. We had done all that we could and it just wasn't enough. That is when the Lord took control of the situation and created a miracle.

God Takes Over the Situation

From out of nowhere, the same officials who had denied his request to be baptized in the hospital changed their minds. After getting over the initial shock, everything was quickly prepared for the most important decision he would make in his entire life. He was baptized in Jesus' name that day, the way the book of Acts commands, and shortly after he died in peace. But before the Lord took him to his final destination, He also had filled him with the baptism of the Holy Ghost, speaking in other tongues, which sealed the deal.

I wrote this long testimony to come to this conclusion: wherever you are in life today, no matter how bad off you are, no matter how many times you have offended God, IT'S NEVER TOO LATE to call on God.

Where you are today in your journey in life cannot negate the great plans God has for you in His kingdom. You are the only one who can actually stop the blessings Jesus has prepared for your life. You really can't use your wasted opportunities as an excuse. We have all failed, and at one time or another fallen down, having made a mess of the wonderful things God wanted to accomplish through us. My God is the only God who can take leftovers and make a magnificent feast from them. It's not how you start that is vitally important, it's how you finish. Look at the list of people below who had a horrible beginning but found the door to their destiny and found the success after so many failed attempts.

Struggling for Success

--The great Italian tenor, Enrico Caruso, was told by his teacher that his voice sounded like the wind whistling through the window.

--When the British statesman, Benjamin Disraeli, attempted to speak in Parliament for the first time, members hushed him into silence and laughed when he said, "Though I sit down now, the time will come when you will hear me."

--Henry Ford forgot to put a reverse gear in his first car.

--In 1902, the poetry editor of *The Atlantic Monthly* sent a sheaf of poems back to a twenty-eight-year-old poet with this current note: "Our magazine has no room for your vigorous verse." The poet was Robert Frost.

--In 1905, the University of Bern turned down a PhD dissertation as being irrelevant and fanciful. It's author was Albert Einstein.

-- The rhetoric teacher at Harrow school in England wrote this on sixteen-year-old Winston Churchill's report card: "a conspicuous lack of success."

-- Thomas Edison once spent $2 million on an invention that proved to be a flop.[26]

I Give Myself Away

The greatest example of perseverance I can give is that of the life of Abraham Lincoln. In all of his attempts to succeed, he had to overcome severe opposition to eventually become the 16th President of the United States.

Difficult childhood
Failed in business in 1831
Defeated for the legislature, '32
Again failed in business, '33
Elected to the legislature, '34
Fiancé died, '35
Defeated for Speaker,'38
Defeated for Elector, '40
Married, wife a burden, '42
Only one of his four sons lived past age eighteen
Defeated for Congress, '43
Elected to Congress, '46
Defeated for Congress, '48
Defeated for Senate, '55
Defeated for Vice-President, '56
Defeated for Senate,'58
Elected as president, '60[27]

If any of these successful people would have terminated their journey to success, we would not have the examples needed to fight through our challenges to the victories God has promised. There are no shortcuts in finding God's will, you can't bypass the process God has used from the very beginning. If we make the decision to follow God's leading, we will have to do it His way and

develop an attitude of submission. We must embrace a "love slave" mentality, and be willing to do the one thing that will bring ultimate success in our walk with God:
I GIVE MYSELF AWAY!

END NOTES

[1] Nathaniel Wilson, *In Bonds of Love* (Sacramento: Reach Worldwide, Inc., 1993), PG 4-9

[2] Merriman-Webster.com/ Dictionary/ diminishing returns

[3] Herbert Lockyer, *All the Apostles of the Bible* (Grand Rapids: Zondervan Publishing House,1972), PG 85

[4] Lockyer, *All the Apostles of the Bible*, PG 88

[5] J.B. Jackson, Dictionary of Scripture Proper Names, Boston, March 1908) Patmos

[6] AllAboutGOD.com/ types-of-angels-faq.htm

[7] Tim Sheets, *Angels Armies, Releasing the Warriors of* Heaven (Shippensburg: Destiny Image Publishing, Inc., 2016), PG75

[8] *The Six-Day War: Recognizing the Miracle* (www.israelnationalnews.com

[9] Miracles in the Six Day War: Eyewitness Accounts, Arutz Sheva (www.israelnationalnews.com)

[10] *The Six-Day War: Recognizing the Miracle* (www.israelnationalnews.com

[11] Merriman-Webster.com/ Dictionary/ inconvenience

[12] Herbert Lockyer, *All the* Apostles *of the Bible* (Grand Rapids: Zondervan Publishing House, 1972), PG 127

[13] Lockyer, *All the* Apostles *of the Bible*, PG 131

[14] Lockyer, *All the* Apostles *of the Bible*, PG 141

[15] Merriman-Webster.com/ Dictionary/ revisionism

[16] Merriman-Webster.com/ Dictionary/ despise

[17] James Nisbet, "Commentary on Isaiah 53:3" // studylight.org/commentaries/cpc/Isaiah/53 html,1876

[18] John Gill, "Commentary on Isaiah 53:3"// studylight.org/commentaries/cpc/Isaiah/53 html,1999

[19] James Nisbet, "Commentary on Isaiah 53:3" // studylight.org/commentaries/cpc/Isaiah/53 html,1876

[20] Albert Barnes, "Commentary on Isaiah 53:3" // studylight.org/commentaries/cpc/Isaiah/53 html,1870

[21] Charles Swindoll, *Jesus:* The *Greatest Life of All* (Nashville: Thomas Nelson Publications, 2009), PG 125-140

[22] Charles Swindoll, *Jesus:* The *Greatest Life of All* (Nashville: Thomas Nelson Publications, 2009), PG 125-140

[23] Passover-Wikipedia

[24] Pentecost-Wikipedia

[25] Article by Christopher Harress - www.ibtimes.com

[26] John Maxwell, *Your Attitude: Key to Success* (San Bernardino, CA: Here's Publishers, 1984). Pg 79-80

[27] Ibid. PG 84

George Pantages Ministries

Books Available in English

George Pantages Ministries
Cell 512-785-6324
GEOPANJR@YAHOO.COM
GEORGEPANTAGES.COM

GEORGE PANTAGES MINISTRIES

LIBROS DISPONIBLES EN ESPAÑOL

GEORGE PANTAGES MINISTRIES
CELL 512-785-6324
GEOPANJR@YAHOO.COM
GEORGEPANTAGES.COM

GEORGE PANTAGES MINISTRIES

CONFERENCIA DISPONIBLE EN ESPAÑOL

9 CD SET

CD 1	SIENDO COMO NIÑOS
CD 2	Cuando Fe No es Fe I
CD 3	Cuando Fe No es Fe II
CD 4	Cuando Fe No es Fe III
CD 5	¿DÓNDE ESTÁ SU FE?
CD 6	Explicando Conceptos de los Dones (I)
CD 7	Explicando Conceptos de los Dones (II)
CD 8	Preguntas y Respuestas (Oración de Impartición)
CD 9	SOLO VAMOS A LA MITAD (Seminaristas del Día Ministrando)

ACTIVANDO LOS DONES DEL ESPIRITU SANTO
GEORGE PANTAGES

NOTAS DE CONFERENCIA

EN

INGLÉS & ESPAÑOL

GEORGE PANTAGES MINISTRIES
CELL 512-785-6324
GEOPANJR@YAHOO.COM
GEORGEPANTAGES.COM